*Black Women Writers
and the American
Neo-Slave Narrative*

Black Women Writers and the American Neo-Slave Narrative

Femininity Unfettered

ELIZABETH ANN BEAULIEU

Contributions in Afro-American and African Studies, Number 192

Greenwood Press
Westport, Connecticut • London

Library of Congress Cataloging-in-Publication Data

Beaulieu, Elizabeth Ann.
    Black women writers and the American neo-slave narrative   :
femininity unfettered / Elizabeth Ann Beaulieu.
        p.   cm. — (Contributions in Afro-American and African
studies, ISSN 0069-9624 ; no. 192)
    Includes bibliographical references (p.   ) and index.
    ISBN 0-313-30838-1 (alk. paper)
    1. American fiction—Afro-American authors—History and criticism.
2. Slavery in literature.   3. Feminism and literature—United
States—History—20th century.   4. Women and literature—United
States—History—20th century.   5. American fiction—Women authors—
History and criticism.   6. American fiction—20th century—History
and criticism.   7. Historical fiction, American—History and
criticism.   8. Afro-American women—Intellectual life—20th century.
9. Afro-American women in literature.   10. Afro-Americans in
literature.   11. Women slaves in literature.   12. Femininity in
literature.   13. Narration (Rhetoric).   I. Title.   II. Series.
PS374.S58B43   1999
813'.5099287'08996073—dc21   98-33756

British Library Cataloguing in Publication Data is available.

Library of Congress Catalog Card Number: 98-33756
ISBN: 0-313-30838-1
ISSN: 0069-9624

First published in 1999

Greenwood Press, 88 Post Road West, Westport, CT 06881
An imprint of Greenwood Publishing Group, Inc.

Printed in the United States of America

∞™

The paper used in this book complies with the
Permanent Paper Standard issued by the National
Information Standards Organization (Z39.48-1984).

10 9 8 7 6 5 4 3 2

This work is dedicated to Sebastian Luke Ivory. I look forward to the day, Sebastian, when you will share your mama's love for this wonderful body of literature.

momma
teach me how to hold a new life
momma
help me
turn the face of history
to your face

—June Jordan
from "Gettin Down to Get Over"

Contents

Preface

In 1849 Ephraim Peabody stated, "America has the mournful honor of adding a new department to the literature of civilization,—the autobiographies of escaped slaves" (Davis and Gates 19). Almost one hundred and fifty years later the study of the slave narrative is thriving. As Peabody anticipated, the slave narrative today is considered an essential component of literary history and viewed as a quintessentially American genre. Scholars labor to authenticate enslaved persons' stories in order to enter previously silenced voices into the record of what it means to be an American. The work appeals to many sides of a scholar—it is historical, it is literary, and it is creative.

But it is also finite. While the works we know of may be debated and interpreted endlessly, and while an occasional new work may be discovered, there is a very limited body of work available for study. We will never know how many authentic slave narratives have been lost, nor can we begin to estimate how many enslaved Americans were never able to tell their stories.

The advent of the neo-slave narrative, therefore, inaugurates a new direction in slave narrative studies. Contemporary fictional works which take slavery as their subject matter and usually feature enslaved protagonists, neo-slave narratives depend on the historical reclamation efforts of slave narrative scholars and contribute to attempts to revise history to include the perspective of enslaved Americans. Important precursors of the neo-slave narrative include Margaret Walker's historical novel *Jubilee* (1966) and Ernest Gaines' novel *The Autobiography of Miss Jane Pittman* (1971).

As a contemporary phenomenon, the neo-slave narrative reflects late-twentieth-century interest in slavery as subject matter. American history textbooks now include the findings of 1960s' revisionist scholarship and thus students receive a more well-rounded portrait of American history. The debate over a national apology for the wrongs of slavery has been rekindled, and there is talk of a national momument to slavery. At the time of this writing, Steven Spielberg's film *Amistad* has just been released, and Oprah Winfrey has just completed a film adaptation of Toni Morrison's *Beloved*. Social commentator and author Michael Eric Dyson observes that slavery is "bursting at the seam of our historical memory" (Alter 60).

I vividly recall my own introduction to the study of slave literature; as an eleventh-grade student assigned to read *The Narrative of the Life of Frederick Douglass, An American Slave*, I barely made it past the first chapter, horrified by Douglass' description of his Aunt Hester's brutal beating at the hands of her master. Who would choose to read such literature? What value could possibly be found in the examination of such wretched lives, in the perpetuation of such stories? Was the explanation to be found merely in the old cliche that those who forget the past are doomed to repeat its mistakes? As much as I came to value Douglass' accomplishment in telling the story of his life in slavery, for a long time I couldn't imagine any writer, and especially any black writer, adopting slavery and its painful legacy as subject matter for his or her fiction.

However, contemporary black writers have embraced slavery, and they have done so with a spirit of celebration. Close attention to the details of everyday enslaved existence becomes a sort of homage to the very humanity of the protagonists and lends to the works a reverence for the past and its attendant hardships. Black women writers in particular glory in the triumph of spirit they find when imagining their enslaved maternal ancestors.

My interest in this study centers around these neo-slave narratives. It has become the project of black women writers who choose to author neo-slave narratives to reinscribe history from the point of view of the black woman, most specifically the nineteenth-century enslaved mother. The writers considered here—Sherley Anne Williams, Toni Morrison, J. California Cooper, Gayl Jones, and Octavia Butler—explore American slavery through the lens of gender, both to interrogate the myth that enslaved women, denied the privilege of having a gender identity by the institution of slavery, were in fact genderless, and to celebrate the acts of resistance that enabled enslaved women to mother in the fullest sense of the term.

The neo-slave narrative as it is being crafted by contemporary black women writers has much to offer our national spirit. By giving us portraits of enslaved life to supplement the extant slave narratives, the writers discussed in this study rearticulate in contemporary terms Douglass' example that enslaved persons were not wretched but instead deliberate, determined, and dignified; by focusing particularly on women who mothered under the conditions of slavery, they give imaginative voice to a previously invisible segment of the American population. These writers reflect an active engagement with America's past and its legacy; they are committed to breaking the silence of the past in order to promote a new understanding. The neo-slave narrative, which leans well into the past for its subject matter and its inspiration, extends the hope of healing far into our future. To paraphrase Peabody, we have the *joyful* honor of welcoming yet another department into the body of American literature.

ACKNOWLEDGMENTS

For their assistance with this work at various stages, the author would like to thank the following people:
—Hortense Spillers, for giving a provocative talk on a February afternoon in Chapel Hill, NC. That talk planted the seed for this work.
—James Ivory, for inviting me to Spillers' talk and for inviting me several months later to be his wife. Thank you for patiently encouraging me through the many stages of this work.

—Trudier Harris, for reading the work in draft form and offering insights, suggestions, and hours of spirited conversation.

—and also Patricia Beaulieu, for a lifetime of love and support.

1

Slavery, Freedom, *Jubilee*: Reclaiming, Repositioning, and Revaluing the American Slave Narrative

When Harriet Jacobs wrote "This narrative is no fiction" (xiii), the words that serve as the introductory statement of the Preface to her *Incidents in the Life of a Slave Girl* (1861), she revealed her awareness that what she was about to relate, the narrative of her life in slavery, had all of the elements of a sensational novel. Rape, willful miscegenation, escape, harsh privation—Harriet Jacobs tells of all of these, and her experiences were not atypical. Black women suffered the greatest indignities of slavery; often forced to work in the fields alongside enslaved males, they were also vulnerable to sexual violation and forced reproduction, and frequently had their children sold away from them. However, the publication of Jacobs' narrative generated little interest in anyone other than abolitionists. The unique plight of the enslaved woman continued to receive scant attention, and she remained an all but invisible figure.

One hundred years later Margaret Walker rekindled interest in the enslaved woman as subject matter by using the facts of her great-grandmother's life in slavery to write an historical novel celebrating black women's endurance. She has acknowledged that even she is unsure of the boundaries between historical fact and fiction in her 1966 novel, *Jubilee*: "When you have lived with a story as long as I have with this one, it is difficult sometimes to separate the two, but let us say that the basic skeleton of the story is factually true and authentic. Imagination has worked with this factual material, however, for a very long time" ("How I Wrote" 62). Following her lead, many black women writers working in the 1970s, 1980s, and 1990s turned to the lives of their enslaved maternal ancestors for stories, the most well-known example being Toni Morrison's 1987 *Beloved*, a best-selling neo-slave narrative[1] based on the 1851 story of Margaret Garner, an enslaved woman who attempted to kill her children (and succeeded in killing one) rather than seeing them taken back into slavery. The facts of Harriet Jacobs' life—the "incidents" she painfully depicts in her portrayal of what it was like to be a black woman in antebellum America—have become viable material for other twentieth-century black women novelists as well, women such as Sherley Anne Williams and J. California Cooper who are not concerned that readers will judge their work merely to be fiction but who are interested in reclaiming, repositioning, and revaluing the black woman's role in America, both in history and in contemporary society. As Deborah Gray White has pointed out, the African American woman "stands at the crossroads of two of the most well-developed ideologies in America, that regarding women and that regarding the Negro" (27).

The ways in which black women have negotiated this "crossroads" are as numerous and as varied as the women themselves. However, in late-twentieth-century African American literature, black women writers have revived Harriet Jacobs' early emphasis on the enslaved woman and have established a new pattern: strong female figures are taking their place beside heroic males, and many of the women are mothers. The re-emergence of the mother figure[2] has lent a new stability to the African American literary tradition by placing the family rather than the individual in the spotlight. It has become the project particularly of the black women writers who choose to author neo-slave narratives to reinscribe history from the point of view of the black woman, most specifically from the point of view of the nineteenth-century black enslaved mother. For Morrison, Williams, and Cooper, as well as Gayl Jones and Octavia Butler, the narrative now *is* fiction, but the testimony of their foremothers is no fiction; it is inspiration.

According to Frances Smith Foster in *Witnessing Slavery: The*

Development of Ante-bellum Slave Narratives, at least 6,000 separate stories have been classified as slave narratives, hundreds of
which were written before the Civil War (ix). But as Charles T.
Davis and Henry Louis Gates, Jr., point out in the introduction of
their anthology *A Slave's Narrative*, "The matter of defining this
genre is complicated by the many novels, printed before 1865,
which imitate the form of the slave narrative, and pretend to be
first-person accounts of bondage in the South" (xxii). Davis and
Gates use this fact to support their contention that the slave narrative as a literary form was widely influential, particularly in the
nineteenth century. However, after the completion of the Federal
Writers' Project targeted to preserve the oral narratives of the last
generation of blacks born into slavery, interest both in the slave
narrative as historical data and in attempts to recreate the form
fictionally waned, although the first-person narrative never completely disappeared. In fact, Davis and Gates argue that, "With the
end of slavery . . . the black seems to have lost his great, unique
theme until Jim Crow racism and segregation recreated it" (xviii).

In *Women, Race and Class*, Angela Y. Davis celebrates the spirit
of those enslaved black women who were never subdued: "[T]hose
women . . . passed on to their nominally free female descendants a
legacy of hard work, perseverance and self-reliance, a legacy of
tenacity, resistance and insistence on sexual equality."[3] Their contribution, she maintains, established "standards for a new womanhood" (29). However, this legacy was not even partially realized
until the civil rights movement in the 1960s. Civil rights and
women's rights bisected in the 1960s in a way unfelt since the days
of abolition. Efforts to secure women's rights had petered out in
the 1940s and 50s, yet the increasing number of women seeking
higher education and the growing desire among Americans for
middle-class status, which legitimized the dual-income family, res-
urrected interest in gender equality. The inspiration women's
groups (predominantly white) took from blacks' struggle for equality provided a new urgency to fuel their own cause. Black women
had more to gain than any other single group from *both* move-
ments, yet their presence continues to be undervalued even today.
Feminist history accords little recognition to their contributions,
and the Fannie Lou Hamers and Rosa Parkses have yet to take
their rightful place beside Martin Luther King and Malcolm X.[4] It

is as if those women, for equally complex social and historical reasons, have been silenced as their enslaved ancestors were silenced. It is my contention, therefore, that the rejuvenated slave narrative is the manifesto of what Davis terms "standards for a new womanhood" (3). The fictionalized slave narrative of the late twentieth century is the inevitable literary outgrowth of both the civil rights movement and the feminist movement, the vehicle directly responsible for revising how we perceive black women and black family relations and for exposing and repositioning the role that gender plays in narrativizing history.

In order to understand the magnitude of the project to reclaim the slave narrative and to speculate as to why black *women* writers in particular have renewed interest in the genre, I wish first to look at historical representations of slavery in America and then at the nineteenth-century slave narrative itself. Necessary to my argument is also a consideration of how slavemasters denied their enslaved females the privilege of having a gender identity by co-opting their reproductive capabilities; to this end I will examine an historical precedent as well as some contemporary theoretical scholarship on gender and motherhood. Finally, following these sections I will address Margaret Walker's 1966 *Jubilee* in detail as a transitional work that anticipates the novels of many late-twentieth-century black women writers concerned with imagining their enslaved maternal ancestors. From the unlikely juxtaposition of the pages of academic history, theoretical scholarship, and the reminiscences of enslaved and newly freed persons struggling for expression emerges one of the most powerful developments in twentieth-century American literature—the neo-slave narrative.

Any declaration of a starting point is necessarily random, but it seems justifiable to argue, as many critics have already done, that Ulrich B. Phillips' 1918 *American Negro Slavery* is the work most directly responsible both for the neglect of the slave narrative as historical document in the early part of the twentieth century and for the perpetuation of a heavily romanticized view of slavery. Essentially, Phillips contended that "slavery in the Old South had impressed upon African savages and their native-born descendants the glorious stamp of civilization" (Davis 3), an attitude that remained largely unchallenged once it appeared in print. It was not until past the mid-twentieth century, again not coincidentally as an offshoot of renewed interest in things black, that historians began to take a revisionary look at slavery. Stanley Elkins' *Slavery*, published in 1959, is still considered a pioneering work but is seriously flawed both in its lack of attention to primary sources and in its insistence on the "Sambo" figure to explain slave personality development. Both male and female historians have criticized the work for its heavily male emphasis, noting that the only status Elkins accorded to enslaved women was their role as mother. Furthermore, his book is now viewed as skewed in its attempt at demasculinizing enslaved males by emphasizing their childlike and feminine qualities.

Whereas Elkins merely left out any complex examination of the roles black women played in slave families, on plantations, and in the work force, scholars generally regard the Moynihan Report, released in 1965 and officially titled "The Negro Family: The Case for National Action," to be one of the most damaging works to the public perception of black women in America. The "matriarchy thesis" it perpetuated still haunts black women and their relationships with men. Daniel P. Moynihan, a Harvard sociologist, asserted that women of African origin are guilty of a sort of "momism"; they smother their men, depriving black males of healthy sex-role development and self-respect. This assessment explicitly linked the economic and social ills of the black family to domineering women and weak-willed men.[5]

What followed were a series of revisionary histories through which the authors attempted to reinstate the black male's presence, both during slavery and afterwards. John Blassingame's *The Slave Community: Plantation Life in the Antebellum South* (1972) revolutionized the writing of history by reclaiming slave narratives, both written and oral, as primary source material. A flurry of other books followed, including Robert Fogel and Stanley Engerman's *Time on the Cross: The Economics of American Negro Slavery* (1974) and Eugene Genovese' *Roll, Jordan, Roll: The World the Slaves Made* (1974). Among the most well-rounded accounts was Herbert Gutman's enormous treatise *The Black Family in Slavery and Freedom, 1750–1925* (1976). What these works have in common is their explicit focus on black men in an attempt to validate them as men. In doing so, however, "women's roles were reduced to insignificance and largely ignored . . . [t]he male slave's 'masculinity' was restored by putting black women in their proper 'feminine' place" (White 22).

In 1981 Angela Y. Davis published *Women, Race and Class*, a work that takes as its subject the American women's movement and the sometimes contentious role that race and class have historically occupied in the fight for gender equality. In her first chapter Davis provides a brief overview of the black woman in slavery. However, she makes it clear to her readers that this is not the primary purpose of her book; rather, in the first chapter of *Women, Race and Class* Davis critiques several of the male-authored histories produced in the seventies, claiming that "[t]hose of us who have anxiously awaited a serious study of the Black woman during slavery remain, so far, disappointed" (3–4).

Since Davis' clarion call, several works have sprung up to fill the void. Among the best, both published in 1985, are Jacqueline Jones' *Labor of Love, Labor of Sorrow: Black Women, Work and the Family, from Slavery to the Present* and Deborah Gray White's *Ar'n't I a Woman? Female Slaves in the Plantation South*. These works challenged prevailing notions of enslaved women as one-dimensional figures capable of little more than rudimentary wifely or mothering roles. In many ways, Jones and White utilized the best of the groundbreaking scholarship that had preceded their work: both texts rely heavily on primary sources, both skillfully integrate the black individual and the black family, and, perhaps most importantly, both works achieve the goal of repositioning the dialogue about slavery to assume a new focus, a focus only hinted at in previous revisionary efforts.

Such works, logical offspring of the intersection of the civil rights movement and the women's rights movement, have had a profound impact on the way we are able to view slavery from a late-twentieth-century perspective. If we take into account the insistence of women such as Angela Davis and the responses of scholars such as Jones and White, our understanding of history and historiography inevitably becomes more well-rounded, and further spaces for inquiry inevitably reveal themselves. The revisionary historical work done over the course of the past several decades motivated black authors; greater factual knowledge of what life was like for enslaved females in the antebellum South prompted a renewed sense of responsibility to *creatively* embody that life more fully. Extant slave narratives from the eighteenth and nineteenth centuries provided the inspiration.

Revising history to reflect more accurately the black individual in slavery was not all that was going on in academic circles during the 1960s and 1970s. Once John Blassingame reintroduced the slave narrative, claiming for it a sense of legitimacy that had been lost since the early third of the century, literary scholars found themselves engaged in an antebellum scavenger hunt. Understanding what their black forerunners had suffered and working to validate their stories[6] provided a new impetus for the fight for equal rights but, perhaps even more importantly, brought to light an entire body of work now considered an essential component of American literary history. The slave narrative became an important document in the black quest for a national identity.

The occasion of Peabody's essay noting the advent of the slave narrative was the publication of the narrative of Josiah Henson earlier that year. Writing for the *Christian Examiner*, Peabody analyzed Henson's narrative as well as those of Frederick Douglass (1845), Lewis and Milton Clarke (1846), William Wells Brown (1847), and James W. C. Pennington (1849). Clearly, even before the midway point of the century, a body of literature existed to such a degree that it could be classified and studied. Peabody's choice of wording is interesting; he accords the slave narrative seemingly equal status among the "literature of civilization," suggesting its great potential for cross-cultural impact.

The battle to claim the slave narrative as a valid artifact has not been an easy one, though. The authenticity question continues to plague scholars. Furthermore, the virtual standardization of the genre has allowed for, even encouraged, generalizations about the slave narrators. James Olney identifies "I was born" as the common starting point for virtually all of the slave narrators and points to a "sameness" that characterizes the six thousand or so extant slave narratives. In an article entitled " 'I Was Born': Slave Narratives, Their Status as Autobiography and as Literature," Olney identifies twelve characteristics of the actual narratives as well as features accompanying the text that, taken together, amount to a sort of "formula" for the genre. Olney's catalogue, as he points out, describes "rather loosely a great many lesser narratives but . . . also . . . quite closely the greatest of them all, *Narrative of the Life of Frederick Douglass, An American Slave, Written by Himself.*" The paradigm he establishes is one of literacy-identity-freedom (Olney 168)—precisely the point at which male-authored slave narratives and female-authored slave narratives diverge.

"I now understood what had been to me a most perplexing difficulty—to wit, the white man's power to enslave the black man. . . . From that moment, I understood the pathway from slavery to freedom" (Douglass 1845 *Narrative* 78). When Mr. Auld forbids his wife to teach Douglass to read, the young Frederick experiences a moment of awareness that shapes the remainder of his life. The "pathway" he understands is literacy, and he determines to obtain it at any cost. Literacy becomes, indeed, his key both to identity and to freedom. James L. Gray, in an article entitled "Culture, Gender, and the Slave Narrative," discusses Douglass' goal in creating himself as the establishment of a public persona. In other words, Douglass downplays any links to family, distancing himself from his blood kin. Instead he validates his self by seeking confirmation of his humanity from others. "This antislavery *spokesman* told the story of his effort to assert the value of his *self* against the restrictions placed upon him and emphasized his separateness and isolation as one way of describing the self and the assertiveness" (39). Learning to read and to write were crucial steps for Douglass in the process of learning to control his own story and, by extension, in confirming his existence and his self-worth by telling that story.

Slaveowners widely believed that an enslaved person who could not read or write was more easily kept under authority. Those who did write could make others aware of the plight of blacks, and those who did read could learn of free blacks and of anti-slave sentiment elsewhere. More importantly, literacy differentiated blacks from whites, masters from slaves. A slave caught learning to read could be punished with additional labor, beating, blinding or even sale. Literacy was a subversive act; to "steal" learning (as Douglass did on the streets of Baltimore) was more threatening to the established white male patriarchy than to steal food for hungry children or trinkets for everyday living. Literacy afforded enslaved persons a greater stake in their own humanity.

But is literacy, as Olney's[7] paradigm suggests, the only means by which identity and freedom could be obtained? In other words, is the only possible triangulation at work in the slave narrative literacy-identity-freedom? Another nineteenth-century narrative suggests otherwise, and its writer practiced a form of subversion at least as crafty as Douglass'.

In "Harriet Jacobs' *Incidents in the Life of a Slave Girl*: The Re-Definition of the Slave Narrative as Genre," Joanne Braxton explores the impact of the inclusion of women's writing on the slave narrative genre, concluding that "[t]he treatment of the slave narrative genre has been one of the most skewed in Afro-American literary criticism. . . . By focusing almost exclusively on the narratives of male slaves, critics have left out half the picture" (380). She argues strenuously for placing Harriet Jacobs' *Incidents* side by side with Frederick Douglass' *Narrative* as the "central text" in the genre (381). Braxton questions the role literary critics have played in canonizing Douglass' account at the expense of others written by women, and calls for further scholarly investigation along the lines of Jean Fagan Yellin's work, which resulted in the 1981 revival and authentication of Jacobs' narrative. She advocates a new emphasis on women's writing and the study of female characters, adding her own hypothesis that the violated woman should be recognized as the archetypal counterpart to the male hero, an observation she elaborates upon in an article entitled "Ancestral Presence: The Outraged Mother Figure in Contemporary Afra-American Writing." In the latter article, Braxton argues that "[f]emale slave narrators like 'Linda Brent' planted the seed of contemporary Black feminist and 'womanist' fiction early in Black American literary tradition" (302).

Harriet Jacobs, in *Incidents in the Life of a Slave Girl*, suggests an alternative paradigm, one representing family-identity-freedom. Here literacy does not play the role it does in Douglass' narrative or life, perhaps because Jacobs had literacy readily available to her, and therefore did not have to scheme to learn as Douglass did. In fact, Jacobs makes allusions to literacy only in passing, in her Preface, for example, in which she begs readers to "excuse deficiencies" (xiii) in her writing, a stock convention of the literature of the time. Reading and writing do not have for her the significance they do for Douglass. Whereas Douglass makes few references to family and friends, these things are at the core of Jacobs' life from the very beginning. Douglass begins his narrative openly acknowledging that he has "no accurate knowledge" (1845 *Narrative* 47) of his birth other than that he was born in Tuckahoe, Maryland, and it soon becomes obvious that he has no sense of family history and, hence, is not able to develop a sense of personal heritage. Instead, Douglass' narrative betrays his thirst for adventure, a motif found in most of the slave narratives. Jacobs, on the other hand, begins "I was born a slave; but I never knew it till six years of happy childhood had passed away" (3). Immediately following this declaration she narrates specifics of her family members, including a lengthy history of her maternal grandmother, as if to suggest that her family was responsible for her early happiness. Her family ties continue to sustain her during her ordeal of hiding at her grandmother's house; although she is uncomfortable physically, Jacobs is soothed knowing she can peek out through a shingle and see her children in the yard below.

Throughout the narrative Jacobs insists on her ties to her family and especially, as she grows into maturity, to her children. Her roles as daughter, granddaughter, lover, and mother confer on her both identity and freedom. Her subversiveness manifests itself in the choices she makes as a woman and as a mother. First, by refusing to yield to her master's sexual advances and by taking a white lover and becoming pregnant, she achieves the near-impossible task of controlling the terms of intimacy; and secondly, by choosing not to run but rather to remain for seven years in her grandmother's attic so that she does not have to leave her children behind, she "mothers" in a way most enslaved women were never able to experience.

The question of an enslaved mother's relationship to her children poses perhaps the greatest contradiction of slavery. Jacobs tells of often wishing for death, but after the birth of her own child she feels "the new tie to life," the apt title of the chapter about the birth. However, as her child grows older she ponders the implications of slavery more seriously, considering not so much her own condition but the future of her child. "Alas, what mockery it is for a slave mother to try to pray back her dying child to life! Death is better than slavery" (62). Jacobs refers to herself continuously as an enslaved mother; not as a woman, not merely as an enslaved person or as a mother. In her life, as in the lives of all enslaved women who bore children, the two roles were painfully yoked.

In *Of Woman Born: Motherhood as Experience and Institution*, Adrienne Rich explores a "cathexis [which is] essential, distorted, misused" and concludes that this is the "great unwritten story" (225); what she describes is the relationship between mother and child.[8] Other theorists, including Nancy Chodorow and Dorothy Dinnerstein, have followed her lead in taking up the relationship between mothers and their children. While these models are useful for most literary studies, they are not entirely appropriate for slave and neo-slave narratives. Perhaps there is no model flexible enough to accommodate slavery and enforced reproduction. Nevertheless, theoretical scholarship on motherhood and gender, increasingly prominent since the women's rights movement in the 1960s, compels our attention to these issues in the lives of the most marginalized of women—slave mothers.

Motherhood is both a social construct and a fact of nature. For slave women it was a paradox. Treated as a commodity, the slave woman's body was frequently colonized by the white master, both to satiate the male's lust and to increase the labor force, since any resultant children would by law follow the condition of their enslaved mother. Deborah Gray White points out that slave women were treated differently from slave men from the moment they were captured and taken from their homeland, often making the Middle Passage not in the hold of the ship in chains but unfettered on the quarter deck. As a result, "they were more easily accessible to the criminal whims and sexual desires of seamen, and few attempts were made to keep the crew members of slave ships from molesting African women" (63). Once in America, enslaved women suffered dual oppression—they worked in the fields alongside their male counterparts, but they were vulnerable to sexual terrorism as well, labeled "breeders" by lascivious, avaricious masters.

The term itself is interesting for what it tells us about prevailing attitudes towards slaveholding. Deborah Gray White points out that the word "breeder" was applied to an enslaved female even by the most genteel, and that slavewomen's reproduction was considered polite dinnertable or parlor conversation (31). What is important to note about the term is that it is devoid of any human connotation. Women were "breeders," as were cattle and horses. In *Women, Race and Class* Angela Davis defines the word as slaveholders used it in strictly financial terms: "animals, whose monetary value could be precisely calculated in terms of their ability to multiply their numbers" (7). Furthermore, when the term refers specifically to a woman it has the effect of completely effacing gender. Davis asserts, "[t]he slave system defined Black people as chattel. Since women, no less than men, were viewed as profitable labor units, [both] might as well have been genderless as far *as the slaveholders were concerned*" (*Women, Race and Class* 5, emphasis mine). A "breeder" essentially has the ability to breed and nothing more; the term in no way implies nurturing or mothering. And yet to breed implies giving birth, something only a female can do, and therefore a function explicitly defined by gender. Hence the biological contradiction of slavery: a mother could not mother.

Not only did it make it easier psychologically to deal in human flesh if that human flesh was not ascribed a gender (or even humanity), but nineteenth-century American slaveholders had a precedent for viewing enslaved persons as genderless. At the beginning of *Politics*, Aristotle writes,

Where then there is such a difference as that between soul and body, or between men and animals (as in the case of those whose business is to use their body, and who can do nothing better), the lower sort are by nature slaves, and it is better for them as for all inferiors that they should be under the rule of a master. For he who can be, and therefore is, another's, and he who participates in reason enough to apprehend, but not to have, is a slave by nature. (1254b15–20)

In a later section Aristotle establishes the male's superiority to the female but makes a distinction between women and slaves: while a woman is "inferior," the slave is a "wholly worthless being" (1454a21). What Aristotle describes is a household unit that comprises the foundation of the social structure, a hierarchy based on three classes—men, women, and slaves—in which the gender of the slave is of no importance. According to Elizabeth Spelman, "For the purposes of a well-ordered state, the distinction between male and female is important only for citizens; for slaves it is irrelevant . . . the distinction Aristotle draws between 'women' and 'slaves' leads to the recognition that for him one's gender identity is inseparable from one's racial identity: only certain males and females count as 'men' and 'women' " (42, 54). Spelman provides a comprehensive analysis of Aristotle's conception of slavery, gender, and personhood, and concludes with a startling insight: having a gender identity is a privilege that stems directly from one's race (55).[9]

Slave narrators use this trope with astonishing frequency. In *My Bondage and My Freedom*, Frederick Douglass says of himself, "I was generally introduced as a 'chattel,'—a 'thing'—a piece of Southern property—the chairman assuring the audience that *it* could speak" (360–61). And later in *Life and Times of Frederick Douglass* he defines slavery as "personality swallowed up in the sordid idea of property! Manhood lost in chattelhood!" (96). Over one hundred years later Toni Morrison places the chattel trope directly in the mouth of the slavemaster in *Beloved* (1987) in the scene in which Sethe overhears schoolteacher say to one of his boys making a study of the slaves, "No, no. That's not the way. I told you to put her human characteristics on the left; her animal ones on the right. And don't forget to line them up" (193).

Indeed, twentieth-century black women writers in particular[10] seem acutely aware of the ways in which enslaved persons were made to seem genderless. Female-authored narratives written in the 1970s, 1980s, and 1990s show a marked preoccupation with mothers—bloodmothers *and* "othermothers"—to use Patricia Hill Collins' term. And in order to claim for their enslaved maternal ancestors their deserved share of fuller humanity, women writers such as Toni Morrison, Sherley Anne Williams, and J. California Cooper have turned to the slave narrative, using it to draw attention to issues of gender, particularly mothering, as they affected the nineteenth-century enslaved American woman. In doing so they have recreated the genre, shifting its focus from literacy and public identity to family. Another shift is obvious—one from slavery to freedom. Unlike the nineteenth-century male-authored narratives, which emphasize a linear progression from bondage to freedom, these women embrace the spirit of Harriet Jacobs, who found freedom without following the North Star.

Twentieth-century slave narratives by black women writers are not so much "slave" narratives—narratives about slavery—as they are *freedom* narratives: stories that celebrate freedom from the "soul-killing effects" (Douglass *Narrative* 58) of slavery, freedom from commodification, and freedom from the invisibility that has historically enshrouded the enslaved mother. By putting the enslaved mother rather than the heroic male at the center of the narrative, writers such as Morrison, Williams, and Cooper have renegotiated the entire meaning of the term "slave narrative"; their neo-slave narratives celebrate triumph not over escaping an institution and its cruel representatives but over finding, recognizing, and claiming one's own "best thing" (Morrison *Beloved* 273). Therefore, the characters emerge not as slaves but as whole women, as mothers capable of loving and caring for their children in spite of the obstacles placed in their way by slavery and slave masters. The resulting works are a decidedly twentieth-century phenomenon. According to Barbara Christian in " 'Somebody Forgot to Tell Somebody Something,' " nineteenth-century novelists "could not be as much concerned with the individual slave as a subject as they were with the institution itself" (333).[11] Late-twentieth-century novelists, on the other hand, are free to present an individual in all her complexities, including her gender. The women who populate Williams' *Dessa Rose* (1986), Morrison's *Beloved*, and Cooper's *Family* (1991) are not genderless beings who work alongside male slaves in the field and feel no emotion for the children they bear. Instead, their stories prioritize gender and especially maternity, and the writers are at work creating meaningful, even subversive gender roles for these characters.

In 1985, in the final section of *Conjuring: Black Women, Fiction, and the Literary Tradition* (Pryse and Spillers), Hortense Spillers meditates on the work waiting to be written by black women and advocates a countertradition that embraces "literary discontinuities" (251) to reflect a multifocal consciousness of African American history.

"Tradition," as I mean it, then, is an active verb, rather than a retired nominative, and we now are its subjects and objects. Quite correctly, "tradition" under the head of a polyvalent grammar—the language of learning woven into the tongue of the mother—is the rare union of bliss toward which African American experience has compelled us all along. (260)

It is my contention that the reinvention of the slave narrative by black women writers in the late twentieth century constitutes the rebirth of perhaps the proudest tradition in African American literature, a "rebirth" responsible for elevating the slave mother from "threefold servitude" (Stetson 67) and from virtual obscurity to a heroic status uniquely her own.

The dynamics of the slave narrative genre rest largely in the interaction between polar oppositions: black versus white, rich versus poor, empowered versus disempowered, enslaved versus free. Margaret Walker, however, writing in the middle of the twentieth century, factors an additional pair into the equation: legally enslaved versus legally free. Her 1966 novel *Jubilee* has an important place in the African American literary tradition; the work may best be looked at as transitional, linking the nineteenth-century slave narratives to the fictionalized slavery and freedom literature of the late twentieth century. Just as the novel straddles two worlds, so, too, does Vyry, Walker's heroine. Raised as a slave in the antebellum South and emancipated by a startling declaration delivered to the Dutton plantation by a Union officer after the Civil War has ended, Vyry spends more than half of the novel ostensibly free but nominally enslaved. Her name itself reflects her liminal position: Vyry sounds like "free," but it also echoes the last syllable of "slavery."

Margaret Walker says of her contribution to African American literature, "I was among the first dealing with characters looking up from the bottom rather than down from the top" ("How I Wrote . . ." 64). Her conception of a female slave as speaking subject is revolutionary. Walker's twentieth-century point of view, informed by her grandmother's stories of family history and the copious material she compiled while researching the novel, coupled with her choice to use a third-person limited omniscient narrator, updates Harriet Jacobs' story of slavery. The bias of autobiography is removed, the abolitionist intention is no longer relevant, and the genre is shaken free from the rigid constraints of form that James Olney identified. However, the freeing of form does not necessarily coincide with a freeing of voice. *Jubilee*, while epic in scale, lacks flexibility, versatility. The plot marches towards its inevitable historical climax; at times, particularly in the second section, history obscures the personal story. In other places Walker's tendency to mythologize Vyry overshadows the personal story; for instance, near the end of the novel she explicitly refers to Vyry as "the motherhood of her race" (407).

Walker says in "How I Wrote *Jubilee*" that her purpose in writing the novel, which took over thirty years to complete, was "to substantiate my material, to authenticate the story I had heard from my grandmother's lips" (56). For her it was a personal quest to better know her own roots, as well as to understand her grandmother's legacy, the stories her father called "all those harrowing tales, just nothing but tall tales" (51). Walker seems to owe a greater debt to Harriet Jacobs than to Frederick Douglass, simply because she followed Jacobs' lead in placing a female protagonist at the center of her slave story. But *Jubilee* has much in common with both Douglass' *Narrative* and Jacobs' *Incidents*: details of a cruel mistress, the protagonist's first severe punishment, daily life both at work and after hours in the Quarters, the thirst for freedom and the despair Vyry feels when the dream seems unattainable. Walker gives the reader ample description of slave auctions (Vyry herself is put up for sale once), public beatings (Vyry witnesses the execution of two enslaved women who were accused of poisoning their masters, along with other enslaved persons as part of the Fourth of July festivities), the ever-present patrollers, and a failed escape attempt. In these ways *Jubilee* stands shoulder to shoulder with the authentic slave narratives, remaining faithful in form and spirit. However, the ways in which Walker revises other conventions of the genre are significant to our understanding of how *Jubilee* anticipates later novels such as *Dessa Rose*, *Beloved*, and *Family*.

In an article entitled "From *Uncle Tom's Cabin* to Vyry's Kitchen: The Black Female Folk Tradition in Margaret Walker's *Jubilee*," Charlotte Goodman speculates on the lack of scholarly attention accorded to *Jubilee*. "Since Walker imitates the conventional linear structure of the traditional slave narrative, perhaps one reason *Jubilee* has received so little critical attention is that it appears to be less innovative than novels like Morrison's *The Bluest Eye* and *Sula* or Alice Walker's *The Color Purple*" (336).[12] But I think that Goodman herself has done a disservice to Walker's work by automatically ascribing to the novel the "conventional linear structure" of "traditional" slave narratives. Four significant episodes in the text illustrate Margaret Walker's break with tradition, a break that is responsible in part for reinvigorating the slave narrative genre.

First of all, the narrative begins not with the assertion, however tentative, "I was born" but rather with the death vigil being held for Sis Hetta, Vyry's mother. In fact, Walker entitles the first chapter "Death is a mystery only the squinch owl knows." Death rather than birth is preeminent in the opening sequence; we meet Vyry only by way of her mother's demise and the one word she speaks, "Mama." In this respect Walker's opening evokes Frederick Douglass. The reader quickly absorbs the poignancy of the young girl's orphaned status and notes the contrast with the happy childhood Jacobs initially delineates; Vyry seems particularly small, frail, isolated, alone—like the child Douglass. In the very first scene Walker reverses a major convention of the slave narrative genre, perhaps to demonstrate not a generic truth (birth) but rather the common humanity shared by the community of slaves awaiting Sis Hetta's death. Granny Ticey's cry signalling Hetta's passing closes the chapter and unites the enslaved men and women in mourning one of their own. "In less than a minute, the death wail went up out of every cabin in the Quarters, and Brother Ezekial began the death chant" (14).

A strong image of family and community emerges at the end of the first chapter of *Jubilee*, and Vyry suddenly seems less an orphan, more the child of each of the enslaved persons. Mammy Sukey and Aunt Sally both function as othermothers, and May Liza, Caline, and Lucy all contribute to Vyry's development once she arrives to serve in the kitchen. Walker reveals her debt to Harriet Jacobs once the first chapter has drawn to a close; in fact, I would argue that the same paradigm identified earlier—family-identity-freedom—is at work in shaping *Jubilee*.

Walker's second significant departure, which reinforces this observation, occurs much later in the novel. A grown woman with two children of her own by the free black man Randall Ware, Vyry—at Ware's encouragement—contemplates running away for the first time. Although he has cautioned her to leave her children behind in order to reach freedom safely and return for them later, Vyry at the last moment takes the children with her as she heads for the river. As Hortense Spillers points out in an article entitled "A Hateful Passion, A Lost Love," Vyry's attempt is doomed from the start:

Her negotiation of a painful passage across the countryside toward the point of rendezvous groans with material burden. It has rained the day of their attempted escape, and mud is dense around the slave quarters by nightfall. Vyry travels with the two children—Jim toddling and the younger child Minna in her arms. The notion of struggle, both against the elements and the powerful other, is so forceful an aspect of tone that the passage itself painfully anticipates the fatefulness of Vyry's move. (303)

Both in presenting a failed escape attempt and in emphasizing struggle, thereby drawing attention to the adventure motif, Walker remains faithful to stock slave narrative conventions. Also, Vyry's inability to ignore her offspring links her to Harriet Jacobs. However, unlike Harriet Jacobs, who chooses confinement in her grandmother's attic in order to be close to her children and to watch over them, Vyry, anticipating Morrison's Sethe, chooses to flee with her children, thereby seeming to demonstrate what today we would consider a more responsible, developed sense of family. In fact, she appropriates Ware's role as decision-maker, acting independently and taking an aggressive role in her attempt to provide the best life for her children.

However, the chapter is charged with gender tension that Walker never fully exploits. She sets up a tradeoff: by masquerading as a man (indeed, the chapter title reflects Ware's command, "Put on men's clothes and a man's old cap") and by following a man's instructions, Vyry stands a chance at freedom. However, to be successful she must do more than put on a man's clothing; she must adopt a man's attitude and suppress her maternal instincts. This proves impossible. The decision to take her children with her is not a calculated one, and perhaps Walker is implying that enslaved females were more impulsive at running than their male counterparts. Vyry surely recognizes the wisdom in Ware's caution against bringing them, but when the children awaken at the moment of her departure, she seems to take this as a sign that they must be together. Knowing Ware will be angry, and aware that they are leaving an obvious trail of footprints, Vyry nevertheless acts as a mother, prioritizing the family life she already knows with her children rather than risking the unknown without them. "I couldn't leave my children; I just couldn't. I knows if I leave my baby she will die" (140).

In this episode motherhood and good judgment seem to be at war with one another. In the following chapter, in which whites capture Vyry and beat her nearly to death, the reader is almost angry with Vyry for following her maternal urge and taking the children on the dangerous journey. It is obvious that Ware's strict warning to leave them behind was indeed, at least from a pragmatic standpoint, right. Masquerading as a man Vyry stood a chance of reaching freedom; as a mother burdened with a sleepy toddler and an infant, her attempt was, as Spillers illustrates, doomed from the start. This raises interesting questions about gender, slavery, and freedom. Is Walker suggesting that only an enslaved woman unencumbered by children had a chance to escape successfully? Does she view Vyry's capture and subsequent beating as a sort of "punishment" for the act of succumbing to a mother's desire, or is the choice of family over self the more heroic choice?

The chapter ends with a convincing maternal image: "Despite everything, she felt glad the children were still with her and they were safe. She looked into little Minna's sleeping face and smiled, and she patted Jim's hand softly to reassure him of her nearness. Then she pulled him closer to her in a warm embrace" (141). However, it is obvious that in this episode Walker betrays some unresolved ambiguities about enslaved women and motherhood. Vyry exhibits characteristically maternal behavior—placing her children's lives above her own—but the cost is great; her act erases her chance for freedom and also results in a severe punishment that brings Vyry to the brink of death. Walker seems to suggest that typical, instinctual maternal behavior is not only inappropriate for enslaved women but also dangerous, but this question receives little development. In fact, this is one of the few episodes in which Vyry's children figure prominently.[13]

Walker's third break from the conventions of the nineteenth-century slave narrative may be interpreted more positively. If in depicting the escape attempt Walker seems caught between the nineteenth and the twentieth century, when she portrays Vyry serving as granny for Betty-Alice Fletcher she is convincingly contemporary in her approach. Jacqueline Jones reports that "in 1870 more than four out of ten black married women listed jobs. . . . By contrast, fully 98.4 percent of white wives told the census taker they were 'keeping house' and had no gainful occupation" (63).[14] Walker uses the opportunity this fact provides to develop Vyry into a more well-rounded character. Although she may be faulted for lapsing in her portrayal of Vyry as a mother, Walker is stronger in her characterization of Vyry as a working woman and a contributing member of her family.

As granny to Betty-Alice and, subsequently, to the community, Vyry recalls an earlier black female character, Nanny in Zora Neale Hurston's *Their Eyes Were Watching God* (1937). Early in the novel Nanny takes Janie on her lap and tells her about life in slavery and the way her own dream had been stifled. In the now-famous statement "De nigger woman is de mule of de world so fur as Ah can see" (14), Nanny expresses the plight of the black woman, forced to shoulder burdens placed upon her not only by whites but also by black men, both during and after slavery. One of these burdens in Nanny's case is the sole responsibility for family.

Ah was born back due in slavery so it wasn't for me to fulfill my dreams of whut a woman oughta be and to do. Dat's one of de hold-backs of slavery. But nothing can't stop you from wishin' . . . Ah wanted to preach a great sermon about colored women sittin' on high, but they wasn't no pulpit for me. (15)

In *Jubilee*, Margaret Walker revises this scene, updating the role of the freed slave woman by giving her a "pulpit," an opportunity to make her presence felt by contributing to society outside the confines of her home. Vyry becomes a "granny" and ministers not only to the black community but also to the poor white women in the town, an occurrence probably not all that unlikely in actuality but, in fact, unexplored in literature. We get a sense, finally, of equality in this chapter—the black and white men raise the house together, the black and white women quilt and chat together, the children play together, and Vyry shares an enormous feast she has prepared in gratitude to her new neighbors. Walker foreshadows this scene earlier in the novel when Vyry and Innis arrive to move into the Coopers' house and onto their land; Vyry recognizes that the poor white family is very hungry and so she cooks up a huge stew and casually offers to share it with them.

I would argue that the "granny" episode is one turning point in the novel. Entitled "I reckon I can be a granny in a pinch," the chapter is short and begins on a positive note, with a "burst of warm weather," "dazzling" days and "shimmering" skies (357). By the end of the chapter, Vyry has successfully delivered Betty-Alice's baby, set straight the myth of "nigger mens with tails" (362), and earned the respect not only of Betty-Alice and her husband and family but of the other members of the settlement as well. One exchange in particular marks the pivotal point, not only in the episode, but also in Innis and Vyry's life. Betty-Alice's mother questions Vyry:

> "What's this I hear about colored peoples? Is you a colored granny?"
> "I'm a colored woman, yes ma'am."
> "Why Lawd! Betty-Alice, the best grannies in the world is colored grannies. They doesn't never lose they babies and they hardly loses they mothers. They is worth more'n money and you is real lucky to had a colored granny." (363)

While a subtle sort of reverse racism is at work here—Vyry is a good granny because she is black—this is the first time in the novel that whites who know Vyry is black receive her favorably. Coming on the heels of the incidents with the Ku Klux Klan, the admiration and gratitude of Betty-Alice and her parents is just the miracle that Vyry has been praying for. Instead of being a granny "in a pinch," Vyry is invited by the white men to accept a position much in demand and well-respected in the community.

This scene also works to reverse some of the negative implications of the escape episode. Once again Vyry stands up to her man, refusing to allow Innis to rebuild and resettle until she deems it to be the appropriate time. Bitter and depressed after being routed not once but twice from her home, Vyry has lost her faith in mankind and trusts only her instincts. This time they do not fail her, leading her to assist Betty-Alice and, finally, to trust the men who come to offer community and protection. Her maternal qualities are highlighted by the profession she has stumbled into; it seems fitting that this former slave woman who wanted to save her children so desperately that she jeopardized her own escape should come full circle and work as a midwife, ensuring the safety of other children and mothers.

In portraying the daily life of a black woman in the antebellum and Reconstruction South, Margaret Walker has privileged the ordinary, the everyday. She says in "How I Wrote *Jubilee*" that, "I always intended *Jubilee* to be a folk novel based on folk material: folk sayings, folk beliefs, folkways" (62). As a result, Vyry, with her soup kettles, her quilts, her soulful spirituals, and her hearty cooking, is emblematic of an entire generation of black women, women whose stories have been, until now, virtually invisible. Hortense Spillers, in "A Hateful Passion, A Lost Love," says of *Jubilee*, "This is a story of the foremothers, a celebration of their stunning faith and intractable powers of endurance . . . it is an interrogation into the African American character in its poignant national destiny and through its female line of descent" (305).

After the reappearance of Randall Ware and the potential conflict that his presence poses, Walker brings the novel to a satisfying close. In the final scene, Walker leaves the reader contemplating the future as well as more sensitive to the past; Vyry is expecting another child. This is not a burdensome pregnancy, as Helga Crane's is at the end of Nella Larsen's *Quicksand* (1928), a sign of entrapment in an endless cycle of motherhood. Rather, it is a measure of her enormous capacity to love and to nurture, the depth of which Walker foreshadows in the granny episode. It is appropriate for *Jubilee* to end on this note of fertility, family, and optimism for the future. Vyry hopes that this child will be a girl, because "Gal babies don't never want to leave they maw easy" (416). Parting with Jim was not easy, as it is never easy for a mother to grant a child independence, but Vyry has the joy of seeing her son go off willingly to obtain education, not sold off as a piece of property, the greatest fear of a slave mother. Finally, Vyry and her family seem truly free from slavery.

The final scene of the concluding chapter represents Walker's fourth significant break from the slave narrative tradition. Ironically, she chooses to narrate the scene not from Vyry's point of view but from Minna's, an indication, perhaps, that Vyry is passing her story to the next generation of women to live and to relate.[15]

Minna cries in loneliness as the reality of her brother's departure for Montgomery sets in. This is the first time that the family has been apart. Through Minna's eyes we see "the big beautiful bed that Innis made for Vyry . . . the high mounds of feather mattresses with the snowy counterpane, crocheted, tasseled, and fringed with white matching shams" and are reminded, as Charlotte Goodman points out, of the first time Vyry sees Big Missy's magnificent bedroom (334). Goodman mentions, too, that Minna has learned to sew and quilt from her mother, thereby becoming an important link in the folk tradition handed down from mother to daughter. She participates fully in the tradition, perhaps for the first time, by presenting Jim with a hemmed handkerchief as a farewell gift. His departure is truly a rite of passage for her.

Perhaps by placing the final scene from Minna's point of view, Walker suggests that Minna feels a hint of the pangs of separation and maternal anxiety that will be her lot as a mother, even though she will not be a slave mother as her own mother once was. Walker demonstrates the inevitable progress of history through Vyry's memories of "hearing Aunt Sally call her back to the Big House and to work" and of the subsequent joy she feels upon reflecting that the hens who "come running when she called" are her own hens, just as her children are her own children: "This time she was feeding her own chickens and calling them home to roost. It was this call Minna heard her mother crooning:

Come biddy, biddy, biddy, biddy,
Come chick, chick, chick, chick!" (416)

The reader can only imagine that it is comforting to Minna to awaken and hear her mother feeding the chickens; it is a scene of domestic tranquility and, above all, stability. Their life will continue with its struggles and small joys, and another baby will fill part of the void created by Jim's absence. The children will work hard, almost as hard as if they were still enslaved, but the family will be proud and self-sustaining, quilting the quilts that keep them warm at night, growing their own food, and raising their own chickens. In *Jubilee*, Margaret Walker has restored to the enslaved woman the right to be a woman of integrity who contributes to her family and to her community with dignity. The narrative ends with the promise that this, too, is Minna's destiny.

Shortly after Toni Morrison published *Beloved* in 1987, Stanley Crouch responded with a scathing review of the novel. Writing in *The New Republic*, Crouch stated, "To render slavery with aesthetic authority demands not only talent, but the courage to face the ambiguities of the human soul, which transcend race" (43). Had Crouch been a mother, perhaps he would have been able to recognize his error in pinpointing the work as a "race" novel. *Beloved* is far more that a novel about what it means to be black; Morrison easily complicates that question. Sethe is black, she is enslaved, she is a mother—and in delineating her character Morrison makes these qualities inseparable in order to pose fundamental questions about the nature of female slavery. Indeed, *Beloved* remains today the most prominent literary signpost at the intersection of race and gender, an intersection that scholars only began to explore in America in the 1960s.

Harriet Jacobs initiated the conversation in 1861 when she penned her account of being a slave and a woman; her narrative, governed by her simple assertion that "Slavery is terrible for men; but it is far more terrible for women. Superadded to the burden common to all, *they* have wrongs, and sufferings, and mortifications peculiarly their own" (79), was the first to depict slavery in gender-specific terms. Almost one hundred years later Margaret Walker renewed the theme, first by researching and documenting her great-grandmother's life and then by publishing the story in *Jubilee*. Walker's contribution to literature—the imaginative recreation of slavery from a woman's perspective and the valorization of folk customs and expressions traditionally associated with black women—cannot be overlooked. Late-twentieth-century African American women writers have adopted and extended her work, continuing to privilege the female slave as speaking subject, but also complexifying her. In particular, a number of neo-slave narratives by women challenge traditional assumptions about slave women; these novels reflect and supplement the revisionary history of black feminist scholars.

In the following chapters I will look at Sherley Anne Williams's *Dessa Rose*, Toni Morrison's *Beloved*, and J. California Cooper's

Family, novels that are responsible for repositioning the black woman in slavery, according her new status as a whole woman with a gender identity completely her own. I will also consider Octavia Butler's *Kindred* and Gayl Jones' *Corregidora* as forerunners of these novels, works that prepare for the radical conceptions of enslaved women to follow. It is my contention that all of these works constitute an effort to rectify the historic invisibility of the enslaved woman by exploding the oversimplified stereotype of black women as genderless work animals capable only of matching a man's work production in the field and of breeding, and by producing viable alternative models of enslaved women, models that continue to inspire black women today.

Hortense Spillers' main criticism of *Jubilee* is that Walker has not allowed herself to experiment. Of the novel she says, "it does not introduce ambiguity or irony or uncertainty or perhaps even 'individualism' as potentially thematic material because it is a detailed sketch of a *collective* survival" ("Hateful" 305). Williams, Morrison, and Cooper have answered this criticism. Just as the female characters have been complexified so, too, have their stories. What the women in these novels have in common is the fact that they are mothers; what the writers have in common is a tendency to utilize subversive strategies such as reversal, blurring, and the creation of myth to dramatize gender identity and to highlight the multifaceted nature of motherhood as enslaved women experienced it. Hélène Cixous says, "Woman must write her self: must write about women and bring women to writing . . . [w]oman must put herself into the text—as into the world and into history—by her own movement" (245). Each African American woman writer who has taken as her project the creation of a neo-slave narrative discovers paradox, ambiguity, and contradiction as she probes the implications of enslaved motherhood; each brings alive the woman who is her enslaved ancestor and the woman who is herself. The result is literature that is personally driven and socially charged, literature that simultaneously honors tradition and creates it.

NOTES

1. This is the term Bernard Bell uses to describe "residually oral, modern narratives of escape from bondage to freedom." See *The Afro-*

American Novel and Its Tradition (Amherst: University of Massachusetts Press, 1987, 289). Bell does little with the term other than providing this basic working definition and using it to label novels such as *Jubilee* and *The Autobiography of Miss Jane Pittman*.

2. The mother figure has always been important in African American literature; consider, for instance, Currer in William Wells Brown's 1853 novel *Clotel*, a character who is genuinely concerned about the plight of her children. I am pointing to a *new* interest, however, in the mother figure in late-twentieth-century African American literature.

3. By the term "sexual equality" Davis refers to the egalitarian spirit that pervaded many slave households; thus, the phrase refers only to the domestic sphere.

4. See especially Angela Y. Davis' *Women, Race and Class* (New York: Random House, 1981) and bell hooks' *Ain't I a Woman: Black Women and Feminism* (Boston: South End Press, 1981) for a more complete analysis of the role black women had in the fights for civil rights and women's rights.

5. Moynihan specifically attributed contemporary social problems to patterns established during slavery, particularly the demasculinization of the black male necessary to keep him enslaved and the dominant role black women were subsequently forced to assume in family life. His observations have been severely undercut, however, by black feminist scholars whose research suggests that black slave households in fact benefited from an unusual sort of gender equality in the domestic sphere. See especially Davis' *Women, Race and Class*, page 17, and Deborah Gray White's *Ar'n't I a Woman? Female Slaves in the Plantation South* (New York: W.W. Norton & Co., 1985, 158–59).

6. Robert B. Stepto provides perhaps the most complete discussion of the difficulty in authenticating slave narratives and the conflicts this task poses to twentieth-century literary scholars in *From Behind the Veil: A Study of Afro-American Narrative* (Urbana: University of Illinois Press, 1979).

7. Other scholars, too, insist on literacy as the essential component in the quest for identity and freedom; see especially Stepto's *From Behind the Veil*.

8. It must be pointed out, though, that Rich's primary focus in this work is the mother-daughter relationship, although her conclusions are largely generalizable to relationships between mothers and all of their children.

9. Spelman's conclusions, as well as the path she takes to reach them, are more complex than I've presented here. See her chapter "Who's Who

in the Polis," in *Inessential Woman: Problems of Exclusion in Feminist Thought* (Boston: Beacon Press, 1988) for further clarification.

10. Black male writers have authored several neo-slave narratives, including *Flight to Canada* (1976) by Ishmael Reed, and *Oxherding Tale* (1982) and *Middle Passage* (1990) by Charles Johnson. Although these novels are worthy of serious literary attention, I have chosen not to include them in my study, focusing instead on black women and their particular negotiation of issues of gender and motherhood during slavery.

11. Christian emphasizes memory as the distinguishing factor, stating that this highly subjective mode of thought "is a critical determinant in how we value that past . . . [b]ut that concept could not be at the center of a narrative's revisioning of history until the obvious fact that African Americans did have a history and culture was firmly established in American society" (333). Hence the neo-slave narrative as a post-1960s phenomenon.

12. Goodman also speculates that *Jubilee* remains relatively obscure because it does not exploit sexism within the black community, a major theme of other contemporary black women writers, and because certain fundamental tenets of the novel (Christian humanism, nonviolence, interracial sisterhood) were contrary to the doctrine of black militarism popular among a certain segment of the black population at the time.

13. There are only two other episodes: when Innis beats Jim and the final scene, the majority of which is narrated from Minna's point of view. I'll be looking at the latter scene shortly.

14. Jones provides an extensive analysis of the freed black woman's employment situation following the Civil War, highlighting the fact that the black woman did not enjoy the luxury of full-time domesticity aspired to and, in fact, enjoyed by so many of her white sisters. Also, she mentions that one quarter of black households, as opposed to 13.8 percent of white households, reported at least one employed child under the age of sixteen.

15. The handing down of stories from one generation of women to the next links Walker's novel with Gayl Jones' *Corregidora*, which I will be looking at in Chapter 5. However, Walker portrays this tradition in a much more positive, healthier manner than Jones.

2

"Cause I Can": Race, Gender, and Power in Sherley Anne Williams' *Dessa Rose*

In an introductory note to "Meditations on History," the novella that Sherley Anne Williams eventually expanded and published as *Dessa Rose* in 1986, Williams says, "I am the women I speak of in my stories, my poems. The fact that I am a single mother sometimes makes it hard to bring this forth to embody it in the world, but it is precisely because I am a single mother of an only son that I try hard to do this. Women must leave a record for their men; otherwise how will they know us?" (198). The record that Williams has given black women in *Dessa Rose* is a crucial part of the revisionary history efforts I noted in Chapter 1; its importance cannot be understated. Williams herself points out in the "Author's Note" accompanying *Dessa Rose* that one of her chief motivations for creating her tale of an enslaved female involved in a plot to rebel was her feeling of "outrage [at] a certain, critically acclaimed novel of the early seventies [*sic*] that travestied the as-told-to memoir of slave revolt leader Nat Turner" (ix). The work to which Williams refers is William Styron's *The Confessions of Nat Turner* (1967), which, in spite of receiving the Pulitzer Prize, aroused tremendous controversy for its use of first-person narration to tell the story of a black slave revolt in antebellum Virginia. One of the primary purposes, then, of Williams' work, is to clarify the historical record.

Williams' work suggests . . . that Styron's interventions result in the misreading of his historical subject, while her own work represents not only an attempt to reconcile the literary treatment to the historical subject but, in the process, to deconstruct her predecessor's methods. "Meditations," then, becomes a gesture of what Henry Louis Gates calls "critical parody," in which Williams revises and thus problematizes the structuration of Styron's *Confessions*. (Henderson "(W)riting *The Work*" 632–33)

In "Meditations on History," and more fully in *Dessa Rose*, Sherley Anne Williams dramatizes the inevitable inaccuracy and incompleteness of black history in the hands of white historians and amanuenses.

Williams' direct challenge of a white male author is not the only way in which she sets out to revise history, however. *Dessa Rose* is an important twentieth-century American novel for the ways in which it calls attention to how black stories are entered into the historical record, but it is equally important for its contribution of an enslaved female voice to that record.

In an interview shortly after the publication of *Dessa Rose*, Sherley Anne Williams explicitly identifies gender and power as the subtexts of her novel. When asked what she intended by having her protagonist declare that she "kills white mens . . . cause [she] can" (13), Williams replied, "what begins to change her [Dessa's] life is the meaning of the possibility of motherhood—her being willing to fight, knowing that she can, that she must, for the life of this child that she and Kaine have created. It's out of that that she begins to push beyond the limits, the very circumstances of her life—so that the first thing is her desire to protect, to have" (Greene 34). Influenced by Margaret Walker's *Jubilee*, in which an enslaved woman is empowered to be the speaking subject of her life story, Williams extends Walker's innovations by prioritizing motherhood in the life of her enslaved female character. In fact, it is Dessa's pregnancy that is responsible for the decision to spare her life at the time of her capture; out of greed for the commodity of the unborn child Wilson, the slave dealer, orders that Dessa remain alive until she delivers her child, who will then belong to him and whom he can eventually sell for a profit.

While it may initially appear that the white male fulfills his traditional role as a symbol of power and authority—indeed, the slavetrader holds power over Dessa's very life—Williams structures the work by means of a series of reversals,[1] contradicting conventional expectations with regard to both race and gender. In the established hierarchy, the white male occupies the highest rung on the ladder of power; in fact, his is the only genuine position of power. White women rank next, commanding respect from white men and blacks alike. Black women, subject to traditional male authority as well as the authority of white slaveowners, assume the lowest position, and black mothers rank even further down on the hierarchy, unable to protect themselves *and* unable to provide for their children. It is my intention to demonstrate that Williams effects a series of reversals that insert blacks into positions of power, thereby questioning America's racial hierarchy. I will also argue that, consonant with her goal of empowering blacks, Williams posits gender equality by similarly elevating women into positions of authority. Williams uses these reversals to imagine the story of an enslaved mother who takes control of her life and her life story against all societal odds. In "Negotiating Between Tenses: Witnessing Slavery after Freedom—*Dessa Rose*," Deborah E. McDowell argues that *Dessa Rose* and novels like it "posit a female-gendered subjectivity, more complex in dimension, that dramatizes not what was *done* to slave women, but what they *did* with what was done to them" (146). In this light, *Dessa Rose* is truly a revolutionary novel. If, as Zora Neale Hurston would have us believe, the black woman is the mule of the world, Dessa Rose belies both her race and her gender, transforming both into agents of salvation rather than of slavery.

Frederick Douglass, in his *Narrative of the Life and Times of Frederick Douglass*, identifies slave singing as "testimony against slavery" (58), and Williams chooses to begin her novel with song rather than expository prose, inaugurating the trope of reversal immediately. The Prologue presents the enslaved persons' own voices, establishing subversiveness from the opening moments of the novel.

Someone . . .
   "Hey, hey . . ."
coming down the Quarters.
   ". . . sweet mamma."
   Kaine, his voice high and clear as running water over a settled stream
bed, swooping to her, through her. . . . He walked the lane between the
indifferently rowed cabins like he owned them, striding from shade into
half-light as if he could halt the setting sun. (1)

   Douglass argues that "[s]laves sing when they are most unhappy.
The songs of the slave represent the sorrows of the heart; and he
is relieved by them, only as an aching heart is relieved by its tears"
(58). Williams revises his estimation of song; even the casual reader
cannot overlook the easygoing, celebratory quality of this passage.
Kaine sings, but his singing is not mournful. Rather, he proclaims
a love song directed to his "Dessa da'ling . . ." (1) whom he has
come to fetch from the fields. In this opening scene Kaine, whom
we later learn works as the gardener on the Vaugham estate, is
presented as a man in charge; he walks through the slave houses
"like he owned them" and possesses a confidence which suggests
that he "could halt the setting sun." In short, Kaine seems godlike;
there is nothing of the slave about him as he "swoop[s]" to Dessa.
   Kaine's singing as he comes to meet Dessa celebrates the end of
the work day and signals the beginning of their time together. His
voice is "high and clear as running water over a settled stream
bed" (1); this correlation with nature evokes a powerful image of
freedom. Furthermore, singing reflects Kaine's refusal to be dehu-
manized. We discover early in the narrative that what sets Dessa
and Kaine apart from most enslaved couples is the fact that they
have freely chosen to be with each other as partners in a monog-
amous loving relationship. As Dessa recalls, "He had chosen her,
brown as she was, with no behind to speak of, and he had wanted
her—not for no broom-jumping mess, but the marriage words"
(58). The element of choice is an important component of self-
determination; Dessa and Kaine are among few enslaved persons
able to exercise this privilege, and Dessa clings to the pride she
feels at Kaine choosing her.[2] In fact, the refrain "Kaine chosed me"
structures much of Dessa's musing as she speaks with Adam Nehemiah under the tree. Although she does not understand his line

of questioning and later reflects that "Talking with the white man was a game; it marked time and she dared a little with him, playing on words" (58), she is open with the particulars of her courtship. In fact, it might be argued that Dessa herself exercises "choice" in her conversations with the white man, choosing what she will reveal to him. The implication may be that Dessa has assumed some of Kaine's independence and self-assuredness after his death.

The opening sequence also foreshadows the call-and-response episode preceding Dessa's break for freedom. Long regarded as a subversive tool that enslaved persons used to convey messages and news to others under the watchful eye of the master or the overseer, call-and-response singing is the vehicle by which Dessa asks, "Tell me, sister; tell me, brother, / How long will it be?" (63) and learns that "it won't be long" before her "Soul's going ride that heavenly train" (64) to freedom. Williams makes no overt narrative connection for the reader, but a careful study of the discursive liberties Dessa takes when talking with Nehemiah reveals her acumen with language and her awareness of the necessity of surviving by wit and craft.[3]

When the novel shifts in locale from the Vaugham plantation to Sutton Glen, Williams has the opportunity to effect another race reversal. At Sutton Glen, a woman is in charge of the estate by virtue of the fact that her husband has deserted her. But Ruth is, in fact, only a figurehead. She is complicit in hiding the runaway slaves who take refuge on her husband's property, not because she has abolitionist tendencies[4] but rather because she needs their assistance in the day-to-day management of her home. Sutton Glen, in the absence of Bertie, is run by and for blacks. Elizabeth Jane Harrison describes the living arrangements at Sutton Glen as "post-pastoral."[5] She argues that, "The absence of men threatens the intact patriarchal structure and allows the development of a different kind of plantation community"(121). It is important to note that when Harrison speaks of the absence of men, she is referring to *white* men, since several black men do, in fact, reside at Sutton Glen. The female-headed plantation stands outside of societal norms, and is a place where no race hierarchy is recognized.

The lack of race hierarchy is perhaps best exemplified by the interracial relationship that develops between Ruth and Nathan.

Whether Nathan's seduction of Ruth is a calculated step designed
to secure her cooperation in the slave-trading con scheme that the
blacks are planning is of little consequence. What is important is
the fact that it occurs. In this relationship Nathan is clearly in
charge, a traditionally gender-appropriate role (the man always
makes the first move while the woman remains demure) but not a
race-appropriate position to occupy. His relationship with Ruth
reverses the dynamics of the relationship he had with his first mistress and lover, Miz Lorraine. Whereas she ordered him to remove
his clothes and knelt before him in order to arouse him so that he
could perform sexually, it is Nathan who "walked into [Ruth's]
bedroom without knocking, closed the door behind him, told her
to take off her clothes" (167). This short passage reverberates with
confidence and power, and in case the reader overlooks the significance of Nathan's role in the seduction scene, Ruth's response
reinforces the reversal: "He spoke with such authority that almost
without thought her hand moved to the drawstring at her bosom"
(167).

Harrison argues that such a relationship can occur only after
property relations have been transformed; in other words, since the
blacks are, ostensibly, equal to Ruth and since they all must work
together to ensure their mutual survival, societal norms governing
relations between blacks and whites no longer obtain. She takes
pains, however, to point out that the relationship in *Dessa Rose* is
far from utopian. Readers question Ruth's motives (as well as Nathan's) for entering into such a sexual union; Williams tells us that
she "used him much as she had Mammy, as the means through
which she participated in the life beyond the yard" (158). And
Harrison points out that the relationship provokes disharmony
among the blacks themselves; Dessa is jealous, and other women
in the small slave community worry about the ramifications if the
master should unexpectedly come home or if a white guest should
arrive unannounced at the plantation. Throughout, the emphasis
is on racial difference; when Harker asks, "What got you so mad,
Dessa?" Dessa replies, "That's a white woman, Harker." The response of the group demonstrates their awareness of the potentially
negative consequences of the relationship: "They all quieted down
when [she] said that" (180). It is interesting to note that Williams
does not posit a happy ending for the interracial couple; at the end

of their adventure together, Nathan goes West as planned, but Ruth, who initially expressed an interest in joining them,[6] goes North.

Ruth allows the fugitives to reside on her property out of necessity, and participates willingly in the slavetrading scheme largely out of self-interest; the plan appeals to her because if it is successful, she will have sufficient funds of her own to return to her family in Charleston with her pride intact. Harker makes it clear, however, that the plan could succeed without Ruth, or any other white person; it is simply that her cooperation makes the undertaking less risky. The reversal Williams effects here is laden with irony; as Dessa herself points out before agreeing to become part of the scheme, "the idea of her, a white person, working for negroes was . . . comical" (197).

The desire among the powerless to unite in order to gain some control over their own lives is not uncommon. Together, the disenfranchised blacks and the white woman deserted by her financially irresponsible husband form a group that in some ways resembles an extended family. It is not until they leave the plantation behind, however, that these individuals are truly able to allow their lives to intersect in such a way that the bonds of true family community can be woven. When describing the relationship Nathan, Harker, and Dessa share, Nathan tells Ruth, "I feels bad for all them that didn't make it. . . . But us three—we did it and we made it. It's gots to be some special feeling after that" (160). What he describes is a feeling of community and shared experience that yokes the three of them. Later, near the end of the con game, Dessa revises her opinion of Ruth, recognizing that Ruth has indeed become a part of the group. "My thoughts on her had changed some. . . . You can't do something like this with someone and not develop some closeness, some trust. And we couldn't help but talk, much time as we spent together" (225). Dessa and Ruth have bonded.[7]

We called up some of the comical things had happened on the trail. She could mock some of them white peoples to a tee and it tickled me even more that she could do this in front of me. . . . Sometimes there in the darkness, I'd catch myself about to tell her, oh, some little thing, like I would Carrie or Martha; and I wondered at her, her peoples, how she come to be like she was. (237)

When the enslaved persons and Ruth cooperate to implement the moneymaking scheme, they realize that trust is an essential element of the scam and that trust can develop only among friends. Furthermore, and perhaps more significantly, both the blacks and Ruth discover the fundamental inaccuracies of racial stereotypes.

The slave-selling scheme that the blacks initiate in order to earn their passage West to freedom is perhaps the richest example of how the white power structure is undermined in the novel. Firstly, Harker appropriates the scam from his master, a gambler who used the deception whenever he found himself in financial trouble. The master is depicted as kind, and one may assume that he never imagined that Harker was studying his example and storing that knowledge for his own benefit later on. Harker's intellectual and practical powers seem superior to the gambler's; he reverses the chiché that "You can't con a con."

More important, however, are the implications of the scam itself. The group of enslaved men and women succeeds in reconfiguring the social hierarchy by placing themselves in a category usually reserved for whites—traders of property. That the property they sell is themselves contributes to the sense of "topsyturvydom"[8] that these accumulating reversals engender. The operation is more daring than any slave escape, no matter how well-planned; whereas running away signals desperation and is largely an emotional reaction to enslavement, this plot to deceive white slaveowners is marked by careful calculation designed to destabilize and reposition the authority of the white male.

Before joining in the plot, Ruth must define for herself a new way of seeing the world and must open herself to the blacks in a way that she has never even considered before. The companionship and, ultimately, the sexual relationship she shares with Nathan is one foray in that direction, but that relationship is problematic in that the intimate terms of their involvement are never fully dramatized. Dessa, then, is the true catalyst of Ruth's transformation. In her response to Dessa's arrival at her home, Ruth demonstrates intuitive goodness. When Nathan and Harker bring Dessa, who is exhausted, feverish, and delirious as a result of her escape and the delivery of her child, to Ruth she acts instinctively to care for both the woman and the baby.

"Go get Ada," Ruth had ordered without hesitation. . . . She shouldn't have done it; Ruth had been over that countless times, also. If anybody ever found out. If they had been followed. But nothing of that had entered her head as she picked her way carefully up the steep back steps, the baby hugged close to her body . . . she could do something about this, about the baby who continued to cry while she waited in the dim area of the stairs for the darkies to bring the girl in. Something about the girl, her face—And: She—Ruth—could do something. (97–98)

Ruth not only offers her own bed to Dessa during her period of recuperation, she also takes Dessa's newborn baby to her own breast and nurses him. The emphasis in this passage is on natural inclination; Ruth acts "without hesitation," and although she may have second thoughts about the prudence of her actions, "nothing of that had entered her head" when she moved into action. Most significant is the urgency she feels—she *could* do something, and so she will. Williams reiterates the scene just a few pages later, drawing attention to the significance of Ruth's act of interracial nursing.

Ruth had taken the baby to her bosom almost without thought, to quiet his wailing. . . . The sight of him so tiny and bloodied had pained her with an almost physical hurt and she had set about cleaning and clothing him with a single-minded intensity. And only when his cries were stilled and she looked down upon the sleek black head, the nut-brown face flattened against the pearly paleness of her breast, had she become conscious of what she was doing. (105)

Ruth responds to an infant, not to color, foreshadowing her tremendous possibility for growth and acceptance. It is, in fact, possible that Ruth's acceptance of Dessa's baby prepares her for her impulsive response to Nathan's sexual advances and prefigures her later involvement with a man of color.

According to Sally McMillen, author of a study entitled "Mothers' Sacred Duty: Breast-feeding Patterns among Middle- and Upper-Class Women in the Antebellum South," most mothers of the period considered breast-feeding an essential obligation, and she documents many cases in which women risked their own health to perform this duty until their milk ran dry. McMillen also records circumstances in which relatives—a grandmother, in one case—served as wet nurses for infants whose mothers were unable to provide adequate nourishment. She concludes that breast-feeding was the preferred nourishment method among antebellum parents, and most would go to any extreme to secure breast milk for their children.[9] "When an infant's life was threatened most families probably used whomever they could find to feed the baby" (351). "Whomever they could find" was sometimes a black woman. McMillen notes that enslaved females who had recently given birth or who had lost an infant were regularly pressed into service, and it was not uncommon for a family to advertise for a healthy black wet nurse. "Available milk, not race, was the criterion" (353).

McMillen spends considerably less time discussing cases of white women nursing black infants, although she concedes that interracial nursing between white women and black children did occur. She is somewhat dismissive, however, linking such instances to overwhelming, inexplicable maternal urges and sometimes greed, if the child was the offspring of an enslaved person the family owned. McMillen sums up her discussion of antebellum white women who nursed black infants by concluding, "a baby's life was at stake, and many mothers probably acted out of a desire to keep any child alive and healthy, whether black or white. Sharing maternal nourishment between white women and black infants was one way some southern women rose above racial prejudice" (354).

However, to argue that Ruth's act of taking Dessa's infant to her own breast is an attempt at overcoming prejudice seems reductive here; Ruth's complicity in allowing the enslaved men and women refuge on her estate and her dependence on them to aid in the everyday operation of her home refute any characterization of her that suggests deeply engrained prejudice. Rather, Ruth interacts with the blacks according to social norms and conventions and seems, many times, confused as to how her relationship with the blacks has come to be defined.[10] When she nurses Dessa's baby, she allows her instincts—maternal or otherwise—to overcome social codes; the act signals her growing courage to be true to her feelings.

Raised to be a prim Southern gentlewoman, Ruth has adapted to life on her own by learning to trust her instincts. Offering shelter to the escapees was the first step; she justifies her behavior, but also meditates on it in such a way as to suggest that she is openly flouting decorum. "[S]he realized that she had fallen into the habit of thinking of the runaways as a slightly malicious means of evening the score in their continuing estrangement in the neighborhood. Somebody somewhere was using the Sutton slaves; why shouldn't she use these—especially since she had neither enticed them away from wherever they came, nor encouraged them to stay here?" (150). The decision to harbor fugitive slaves is a dangerous one, yet it is one that demonstrates Ruth's subversive desire for power. Nursing the black infant is another way of flouting convention. Ruth again obeys her instinct, choosing to preserve life rather than to embrace societal norms and the prejudices they cultivate. It is no accident that Ruth feels delight at nursing the baby; "[w]hatever care she might have had about the wisdom of her actions was soon forgotten in the wonder she felt at the baby" (106). Ruth's "adoption" of Dessa's baby also prepares her for the role she will take in the slavetrading scam and for her eventual recognition of the fundamental inhumanity of slavery—an awareness that will redirect the course of her life.

Ironically, in a display of reverse prejudice, it is Dessa who strongly objects to having a white woman nurse her child. As she begins to recover, Dessa realizes that she has little milk and is aware that someone else is caring for her infant. In a dreamy haze she contemplates the change in her life's circumstance: "Runaways. Ada, Harker, how many others? And the white woman let them stay, nursed—Dessa knew the white woman nursed her baby; she had seen her do it. It went against everything she had been taught to think about white women but to inspect that fact too closely was almost to deny her own existence" (123). Later, as she grows stronger and more aware, Dessa feels a void at not being able to nourish her own child. "It hurt me to my deepest heart not to nurse my baby. Made me shamed, like I was less than a woman. And to have him nursing on her. . . . Oh, I accepted it. Wasn't no choice; but I never did like to see it" (183). Dessa's reaction intensifies the resentment she feels towards Ruth, due, perhaps, to what she perceives to be the white woman's appropriation of her responsibility to nurture her child and her own powerlessness.

The reversals I have noted thus far all find their origin in racial politics; as I have illustrated, the novel problematizes the accepted stereotype of blacks as powerless by presenting a number of situations in which blacks exercise power over whites. It is my contention that these examples of power reversal serve primarily to call attention to a reversal Williams envisions that is perhaps more subtle. By the conclusion of *Dessa Rose*, it is obvious to even the most casual reader that this is a story of a woman's triumph in a (white) man's world.

Initially, the novel situates Kaine and Dessa as equals; their love is portrayed as the overriding force in their lives. Although their work roles are reversed in terms of conventional gender expectations—Dessa works in the fields; Kaine is a house slave—this was not in itself an unusual arrangement during slavery. However, this reversal provides Williams with the occasion to depict Kaine as a nurturer. In two specific instances Williams characterizes Kaine as performing duties normally associated with mothers: cooking dinner for the family and singing a lullaby. Greeting Dessa in the field at the end of the workday, Kaine tells her that he has convinced Aunt Lefonia to give him some beef from the House. "And I pulled some new greens from out the patch and seasoned em with just a touch of fatback" (3). Later in the evening Kaine sings Dessa to sleep, soothing her after her many hard hours of labor. Dessa recalls their nightly ritual: "I be laying up on our pallet and he be leaning against the wall. He play sweet-soft cause he say that what I needs, soft-sweeting put me to sleep after I done work so all day" (32). Such domestic equality was an anomaly, because although performing chores around their own homes provided the only meaningful labor for enslaved persons to engage in (A. Davis *Women, Race and Class* 17), "a strict sexual division of labor in the quarters openly challenged the master's gender-blind approach to slave women's field work" (J. Jones 29). Williams goes to great extremes, then, to call attention to the relationship Kaine and Dessa share. The emphasis on choice and the role reversals both in assigned labor and in domestic roles suggest early in the narrative that the disempowered will not be portrayed as such, and they certainly will not act as such.

Williams also depicts the men who accompany Dessa on the coffle as nurturing.

There was no set moment when she knew that the negro driver the white men called Nate was paying attention to her or that the young mulatto boy who often walked the chain in front of her was being kind. Gradually she realized that she never stumbled when the mulatto walked in front of her, that there was always something extra on her plate—a bit of home-fry when everyone else had only grits, a little molasses for her bread. . . . Dessa knew herself to be enveloped in caring. (57–58)

These men genuinely care for Dessa, offering her physical comforts, extra food, and conversation to sustain her on the journey. Cully whispers with her at night and sometimes touches her expanding stomach, "marvel[ling] that the baby moved" (58). The food they sacrifice for her is nourishing, but more important is the way they work to affirm her spiritual and emotional existence, trying to draw her out of her silence and into the folds of their community. Perhaps they pity her on account of the harsh treatment she has received physically and emotionally at the hands of her master, but their care for Dessa extends beyond pity. The men seem to recognize that Dessa's scars are only the beginning of her ordeal, and are sensitive to the sorrow that awaits Dessa when she becomes an enslaved mother to an enslaved child.

That motherhood was a trial but also a cause for celebration among enslaved women is a theme that resonates throughout *Dessa Rose*. Early in the text Dessa recalls what seems to be the only real disagreement of substance between her and Kaine. When she discovers that she is pregnant, Kaine orders her to go to Aunt Lefonia and terminate the pregnancy, rationalizing that "Masa'd sell off any youngun on the place as soon as look at em cause he know we can always make another one" (45). For Kaine, denying the white master any more slaves to increase his wealth and labor force is one small means of achieving power. For Dessa, however, the unborn child is the tangible presence of the love she and Kaine share, and is all the more precious because they have few tangible possessions. Later, when the baby is born, Dessa rejects the suggestion that she name him after Kaine, repudiating the past and all its painful memories. "The baby's daddy, like that part of her life, was dead; she would not rake it up each time she called her son's name" (159). The child becomes for Dessa the totality of her existence, pointing back to her enslavement and the period of her greatest loss, but also looking forward, for Mony is Dessa's reason to strive for freedom, a dream she thought died when the master killed Kaine. Once Kaine dies Dessa assumes the central role in the story and becomes responsible for her own fate. Her position in the narrative is immediately revised; no longer is she the field girl whose brave, easygoing, and generous husband dotes on her; rather, she is a rebel, a renegade slave, the "debil woman" who viciously attacked her mistress and then the leader of the coffle she was sold to, injuring the former and killing the latter. She is also a mother, a fact that seems to contradict all of these other roles.

"Who would think a female that far along in breeding capable of such savagery?" (13) wonders Adam Nehemiah when he meets Dessa and learns her story. Indeed, Dessa's pregnancy poses interesting questions about slavery, motherhood, and power. Why, for instance, does Sherley Anne Williams imagine a pregnant protagonist? Surely the fact that Dessa is expecting a child has more narrative and thematic relevance than simply the fact that it is the reason the slavetrader delays her execution. It is my contention that impending motherhood provides Dessa with a spirit—a power— that Kaine did not have. Kaine allowed the master to break his spirit along with his banjo, something Dessa never fully reconciles. As I have indicated, she fights for the child even before it is born; perhaps the baby offers to her the promise of new life and hope for the future, an extraordinarily precious commodity for enslaved women and one that Dessa would fight extremely hard to preserve. The senseless death of Kaine and the anticipation of his child combine to instill in Dessa a tremendous will to survive. "I knowed what had killed Kaine, the master's power" (187), reflects Dessa. That knowledge empowers her and she begins to understand that if she can coopt some of "the master's power" and combine it with her own will, she will improve tremendously her chances of freeing herself and Kaine's child. Whereas Vyry in *Jubilee* dressed in a man's cap and a man's old clothes to sneak away from the plantation, Dessa's emancipation results from her brutal fighting, two daring escapes and then, ironically, her act of cooperation with a white woman. The novel further demonstrates that Dessa can move beyond her early statement, "I kill white mens cause the same reason Masa kill Kaine. Cause I can" (13). What is most astonishing about the story that Williams dramatizes is the fact that motherhood provides the inspiration and motivation for Dessa's emancipation; she succeeds in liberating herself both because of and in spite of being pregnant, and then being the mother of a newborn child.

Ruth is a bit awed by Dessa upon meeting and getting to know her. She recalls that her son Timmy told her that the other blacks refer to her as "debil woman" and she wonders how Dessa could have acquired such a nickname. Ruth herself recognizes Dessa's fighting spirit and admires it. "She would not admire the action—one couldn't, of course, approve any slave's running away or an attack on a master—still, something in her wanted to applaud the girl's will, the spunk that had made action possible. The wench was nothing but a little old colored gal, yet she had helped to make herself free" (158). Ruth possesses the insight to perceive that Dessa, as a fugitive slave, is freer than she herself is; soon after meeting Dessa, Ruth reflects on her own station in life: "She would have no more rights than they [the blacks] when Bertie came back" (162). It is this awareness of her fundamental lack of power that motivates Ruth to join the blacks in their con scheme, something she perceives as a way to provide for her own security, and a means by which to more actively subvert traditional norms of power than by merely allowing some fugitives to live on her husband's land.

That powerlessness as a result of one's gender identity is a stronger unifying force than race is a dividing one is the revolutionary perspective that Sherley Anne Williams offers in *Dessa Rose*. The bond that develops between Dessa and Ruth arises largely because they are women sharing a subordinate position in society. Ruth Sutton's story parallels Dessa's, drawing attention to the fact that gender inequality in antebellum America had little to do with race. Both women are alone, surrounded by no family other than their children. Both feel the absence of their husbands profoundly, Dessa because Kaine became her family and the love they shared was immediate and real, Ruth because Bertie heralded the promise of an exciting new life for her, fathered her children and then left her, emotionally abandoned and financially insecure. Two scenes in particular work to reverse the conventional expectation that a woman—whether black or white—in nineteenth-century America was powerless without a man by her side. Before looking at the relationship that develops between Dessa and Ruth, however, it is necessary to consider briefly two other females in the novel, black women who have minor roles in terms of the overall plot but whose actions have an irreversible impact on Dessa's life and freedom.

The first is Jemina, Sheriff Hughes' cook, who with her husband tends to Dessa while she is imprisoned in the root cellar. In the short amount of time that she can spend with Dessa each day, Jemina shares gossip and news, and chuckles with Dessa when she tells her that she has been nicknamed "debil woman" by the whites whom she terrified during the uprising. In this way she provides Dessa with support and encouragement during her confinement, bolstering her spirits and keeping her in touch with the black community. But what she offers Dessa goes beyond the boundaries of female friendship. It is Jemina, Hughes' trusted family servant who had been with his wife since childhood, who is responsible for freeing Dessa when Nathan and Harker arrive to assist in her escape. Jemina not only subverts her master's authority, but she is a good actress as well. "Hughes' darky was, of course, incoherent— when was a nigger in excitement ever anything else?—but we finally pieced together, between the darky's throwing her apron over her head and howling, 'Oh, Masa, it terrible; they was terrible fierce,' and pointing to her muddied gown to prove it, what must have happened" (70). Jemina represents the hundreds of anonymous enslaved men and women who did what they could to help another enslaved person escape, even at the risk of jeopardizing their own well-being.

Although we never hear of Jemina again in the text, she is mirrored near the end of the novel in the person of Aunt Chole, the old black granny whom the sheriff authorizes to look at Dessa's scars in order to prove her identity. The old woman, like Jemina, risks her life and her credibility to lie for Dessa: "I ain't seed nothing on this gal's butt. She ain't got a scar on her back" (254), she reports, ironically confirming Nehemiah's racist charge that, "You can't set no darky to check a darky, catch a darky. That's the mistake they made at the last place" (253). Presumably Aunt Chole has been called to perform this "service" for the sheriff before; she comes prepared with drapes to hang around the cell to ensure privacy, and she accepts Dessa's offer of a small coin as payment rather routinely. Most significantly, the narrative betrays no hesitation on her part to lie in order to save Dessa; in fact, it seems from the start that she has little interest in looking for the whipmarks but instead is practiced at keeping up the pretense. The fact that the sheriff trusts her is a measure of how powerful a woman she is. I would argue that Aunt Chole is, then, the embodiment of the *potential* that Jemina demonstrates in freeing Dessa from the root cellar. Together, Jemina and Aunt Chole are responsible for Dessa's delivery into freedom, not once but twice, and it is no coincidence that her safety was ensured each time by a strong black woman who demonstrated courage in the face of patriarchal power.

The first scene in which Williams consciously draws attention to gender reversal occurs when Dessa and Ruth are on the road working the con scheme together. On the first night the group pulls up to "a sizable plantation" (214) and its owner, Mr. Oscar, offers them his hospitality. It is the first time that Dessa and Ruth get to try out their roles, and each stumbles a bit, making minor errors that Mr. Oscar apparently fails to notice. Indeed, the plantation owner seems to have his eyes elsewhere, and it becomes apparent that he hopes to seduce Ruth. Helping Ruth dress for dinner, the equality of the two women—bound as they are by the scheme—is dramatized in a small scene in which Dessa comments that the outfit Ruth has chosen to wear is too formal for the occasion; "This seem more like what Harker said you should wear" (216), Dessa tells Ruth, illustrating her allegiance to Harker as their leader and her own insight into the appearance of things. After Ruth overrides her suggestion, Dessa helps her get ready and settles down to sleep.

When the women awaken later in the night to find Mr. Oscar in their bedroom, attempting to get into Ruth's bed, it is the first time that they have had to deal with crisis together. And the two make a wonderful team; the scene in which Dessa and Ruth attack the drunken plantation owner with feather pillows is one of the funniest in the book. After the danger has passed and Mr. Oscar has crawled out of the room, banished by his own pillows, the women break into uncontrollable laughter. It is a significant moment of bonding for Dessa and Ruth; together they have triumphed over a white male, a task neither would have been likely to have accomplished on her own. The event takes on further significance when Ruth gestures for Dessa to join her in the comfortable bed rather than resume her position on the pallet on the floor. This was how the two women slept when Dessa was first brought to Ruth's for safety and recuperation, and is a further sign of the equality the two women share now that they are partners in the con scheme.

Dessa does not sleep immediately, though, and instead reflects on the new awareness the night's events have given her. "The white woman was subject to the same ravishment as me; this the thought that kept me awake. I hadn't knowed white mens could use a white woman like that, just take her by force same as they could with us" (220). In this episode, Williams revises and updates one of the primary themes of Harriet Jacobs' *Incidents in the Life of a Slave Girl*. Feeling guilty over her efforts to control the terms of intimacy in her own life, Linda Brent argues that "slave women ought not to be judged by the same standard as others" (56). Here she makes a distinction between black and white women. However, Dessa offers a more enlightened perspective, recognizing after the incident with Mr. Oscar that women of all races are essentially powerless. Instead of reporting Ruth's poor judgment in dress and behavior to Harker as she had originally planned to do, Dessa keeps quiet.

> I wasn't so cold with her no more . . . now it was like we had a secret between us, not just that bad Oscar . . . I couldn't bring myself to tell Harker, neither Nathan about that night. Seemed like it would've been almost telling on myself, if you know what I mean. . . . But really, what kept me quiet was knowing white mens wanted the same thing, would take the same thing from a white woman as they would from a black woman. Cause they could. I never will forget the fear that come on me when Miz Lady called me on Mr. Oscar, that *knowing* that she was as helpless in this as I was, that our only protection was ourselfs and each others. (220)

Three points stand out in this passage. The first, that telling on Ruth would be like telling on herself, indicates how closely Dessa has identified with Oscar's attack on Ruth. The second, the recurrence of the "cause they could" motif, signals powerlessness, but in this situation it is powerlessness as a result of gender, not race, an important thematic move that revises the overall message of the novel. And finally, Dessa and Ruth are not powerless in this scene; because Dessa recognizes that the "only protection was ourselfs and each others," the women succeed in overcoming Oscar by disregarding race and acting cooperatively. This scene prepares Ruth and Dessa in an important way for their future adventures together and especially bonds them in a shared sisterhood, readying them for the test they will face in the climax of the novel.

The novel contains a second scene in which the two women work together to subvert patriarchal authority, and this scene is perhaps more significant in that Dessa's liberty is at stake. Williams foreshadows the episode in an earlier conversation that Ruth has with Nathan, querying him about what occupations the blacks who live on her estate have had. Nathan jokes extensively with her, and Ruth joins in the bantering, although she recognizes that "she doubted she understood half of what was going on" (164). When the discussion turns to what the enslaved women were required to do, Nathan quickly loses his joking manner and becomes serious. " 'Well,' he said. 'You know womens don't never have such a good time as the mens' " (164). Ruth does not pursue the conversation; instead, an awkward silence develops between them, presumably as each contemplates the reality of Nathan's statement. Left unclear, however, is whether or not Ruth is indeed aware of the plight of enslaved females.[11]

After seeing Dessa's scars and after her own frightening experience with a white male, Ruth is a changed woman, ready to defend Dessa in front of the sheriff and Adam Nehemiah in the showdown that serves as the novel's climax. Ironically, to do so Ruth must play up her femininity to obtain the upper hand; she exhibits womanly charm, "dimpl[ing] her way" and using "big eyes and quick smiles" (246), acting flirtatious to position herself in such a way that the sheriff must abide by the unwritten code that governs a Southern gentleman's conduct.

"Sheriff, what is this nonsense about my girl?" Sheriff come to his feet; even Nemi stood up. . . . She had Clara in her arms, petting her back like she was pacifying her but she looked some upset. "Is somebody trying to steal Dessa? Is that what he was trying to say? It's just scandalous how peoples will prey on defenseless womens." . . . Sheriff hurried round his desk. . . . "Ma'am," touched his hat, "beg pardon, ma'am." (248)

Ruth is clearly in charge when she speaks with the sheriff, but is less so in her exchanges with Adam Nehemiah. He catches her off guard because she is, quite frankly, shocked at the allegations (some of which she recognizes as true) he makes about Dessa. When he insults her womanhood, however, by daring to ask if she would lie, she regains her posture of authority. "Well, she drawed up at that; white man ain't posed to call no white lady a lie. 'Sheriff, who is this person?' " (249). When Dessa interrupts to tell Ruth that Nemi has similarly accused other black women and has made them undress, Ruth acts the part of the outraged female: "Her eyes flew open at that and the sheriff turned red when she looked at him" (249–50). He himself apologizes and orders Nehemiah to do so as well.

Ruth's "power" in this scene rests largely in her ability to conform to and manipulate societal dictates concerning how a lady should behave and in her newfound confidence. Dessa, however, wields a different kind of power in the climax of the novel. Although Nehemiah does pose a very real threat, Dessa revises the image of him that both Ruth and the reader receive. In particular, she reverses the animal imagery that Nehemiah used to characterize her in their earlier meetings.[12] As she waits to find out what her fate will be, Dessa records her impressions of the white man in terms of animal images, a significant repositioning of one of the stock conventions of slave narratives. She describes him by saying, "He looked plumb wild, way he was throwing his head back like a horse and brushing at that hank of hair" (246), and later she draws an analogy between Nehemiah on her trail and a bloodhound (247). Furthermore, her narrative perspective calls attention to details that delegitimize Nehemiah and make him appear a "trifling little white man" (247).

I looked at his ankles showing gray and bony above his low-top shoes . . . his shirt don't even have no collar; his ankles dirty. . . . See, this had been a precise white man; even when he took his coat off, his sleeves was rolled just so. He'd sweated; you couldn't help but sweat, not in that heat. But, I mean: The sweat did not bead; it wouldn't roll down his face. And here he was sitting up here with no hose on his feet. (247)

Dessa consoles herself with the knowledge that Nehemiah has become disheveled and she notes that the sheriff even seems to treat him disdainfully. It is interesting to note that both the sheriff and Dessa refer to Nehemiah now as "Nemi," the diminuative of his more imposing name. "They couldn't take the word of no white man like that, not against the word of a respectable white lady" (247). Mae G. Henderson, in "(W)riting *The Work* and Working the Rites," argues that Adam Nehemiah has become obsessed with Dessa to the point of infatuation and cites convincing textual evidence to support her claim. If this is the case, then Dessa's objectification of him during their showdown at the sheriff's office is indeed a dramatic reversal, one in which she exercises precisely the same type of power over him that he used in their conversations in the root cellar. Dessa even wishes that she could make him "smell himself" (252), just as he made her aware of her odor by placing a handkerchief over his nose whenever he spoke with her.

"The white man was crazy; I'd make them see that" (248). Dessa does, in fact, succeed in directing Ruth's attention to Nehemiah's questionable appearance. Ruth, in turn, convinces the sheriff that Dessa must be examined in private, obviously willing to take her chances with the old granny rather than the white male patriarchy. Furthermore, even the baby girl, Clara, has a hand in challenging Nehemiah's authority, scattering the pages of his work, most of which prove to be blank, all over the jail when she knocks the manuscript away from him. In his rage at being exposed and undermined, Nehemiah lashes out broadly: " 'You-all in this together'—grabbing at us—'womanhood' " (255). Although Dessa's greatest fear was "be[ing] brought so low by such a trifling little white man" (247), in fact, it is Nehemiah who is "brought low" as a result of the collaboration of women.

Dessa and Ruth bridge the final gap in their relationship once they leave the jail; they are friends. Only a few short hours before the encounter with Nehemiah, Dessa could not comprehend the fact that Ruth could possibly be sincere in wishing to extend the boundaries of their relationship in that direction. "Like I don't know friend from slave just cause I spoke up about Nathan. I had swole up when Martha spoke about that Robert boy, how he bragged on the girls before the mens. I membered that and it was like a pain in my heart. That was what the white woman was talking about, being Martha, being like Carrie to me; and I was shaken" (240). Dessa admits that "the white woman I'd opened my eyes to at the start of the summer wasn't the one I partnered with on that journey" (240), but significantly, she is still "that white woman." However, when they leave the jail together, partners not just in the con scheme but in subverting patriarchal law, each corrects the other's misnaming. "I was about bursting with

what we'd done and I turned to Miz Lady. 'Mis'ess,' I said, 'Miz—'
I didn't know what I wanted to tell her first" (255). Dessa stumbles
because she recognizes that the terms she previously used to refer
to Ruth no longer obtain, and Ruth is quick to come to her aid.
" 'My name Ruth,' she say, 'Ruth. I ain't your mistress' " (255).
Dessa is then liberated to tell Ruth that her name is "Dessa. Dessa
Rose. Ain't no O to it" (256). Clearly, she does not want Ruth to
misname her in the same way that the white man did.

When the women call each other's name simultaneously, the pact
is sealed—each has chosen friendship over race. They wish to hug
publicly but recognize that theirs is a bond that society does not
embrace. In the Epilogue Dessa reflects on the telling of her story,
a story she ensures has been written down and repeated to her so
that she can be sure that her life will not be misread, misnamed or
misappropriated again. Hers is a legacy for the children: "I hope
they never have to pay what it cost us to own ourselfs. Mother,
brother, sister, husband, friends" (260).

Dessa's final reminiscences underscore two important thematic
concerns of the novel; first, Dessa's struggle was to "own" herself,
the ultimate achievement for a black person in nineteenth-century
America, and possible only by rejecting subordinate status and ap-
propriating some of the power the white male reserved for himself
and those like him. And secondly, in her struggle to liberate herself
for the "children," Dessa comes to the awareness that interracial
friendship is possible, and that when she allowed it to happen, it
was a beautiful thing. Elizabeth Schultz posits that "Women characters in novels by black women come to appreciate one another
as individuals, as women, as members of different races or the
relationship dissolves" (75). This is an apt characterization of the
friendship that Dessa and Ruth finally enjoy. Although Ruth does
not join the blacks when they head West, she figures prominently
in Dessa's closing reverie; we can assume that she is first among
the "friends" Dessa recalls along with the family members she lists.
Just one year after Schultz's conclusion that "Repeatedly in the
novels of black women . . . interracial friendships are interrupted
by a racial power play on the part of the white woman" (75–76),
Williams contradicts her statement, offering *Dessa Rose* as a tes-
tament to the possibilities that interracial friendships extend to
women of all colors.

Adam Nehemiah ends one of his journal entries with the conclusion that, "Truly, the female of this species is as deadly as the male" (39). In depicting Dessa as an enslaved female *and* as a mother, Sherley Anne Williams deconstructs Nehemiah's statement in such a way that, by the end of the narrative, it resonates with possibilities extending far into the African American community. Initially, Nehemiah's allegation seems to place Dessa in the company of Sethe, the heroine of Toni Morrison's 1987 best-seller *Beloved*, who is completely unable to reconcile the emotional demands of motherhood and the dehumanizing effects of slavery. In an article entitled "The Structuring of Emotion in Black American Fiction," Raymond Hedin argues that "[t]he narrative dilemma posed by anger became worse for black fiction writers than it was for slave narrators. For the inclination to express anger and to see it as an essential element in black humanity has increased, while the felt need to mute its expression and to provide counterbalancing signs of rationality and control has not diminished" (40).[13]

Sherley Anne Williams is particularly successful in balancing the rage that must, by virtue of her treatment and her imprisonment, consume Dessa. Nehemiah is not far off the mark when he describes Dessa as "a wild and timorous animal" when he meets her in the root cellar. But Williams does not allow Dessa to remain static, and Dessa's rediscovery of her human side, one of the most moving aspects of the novel, is able to occur largely because she is a mother. Patricia Hill Collins, in her article "The Meaning of Motherhood in Black Culture and Black Mother/Daughter Relationships," posits that "the experience of motherhood can provide Black women with a base for self-actualization, status in the Black community, and a reason for social activism" (4). Although she makes this claim for contemporary black women, Collins' assertions hold true for their foremothers as well. Dessa is "deadly" precisely because she is a mother; in this novel, motherhood is the ultimate type of power.

Reflecting on Cully, one of the enslaved men who had been on the slavetrader's coffle with her, Dessa muses, "[h]e might as well been carried in a bottle for all he knowed" (182). The metaphor, which comes midway through the novel, is a bit of an anachronism. It is grounded in our twentieth-century awareness of test-tube babies and in-vitro fertilization, yet it refers simply to a slave to whom "Mammy wasn't no more . . . than breast in the night" (182). Williams uses the metaphor of the bottle-womb to bridge the gap between her twentieth-century audience and her subject matter, forcefully underscoring the point that enslaved motherhood was an oxymoron and dramatizing both what black women have overcome[14] and what they have become. My reading, which emphasizes reversals that empower blacks, women, and, most especially, black women, lends added significance to the title of the novel. "Dessa Rose" becomes not only the protagonist's name and her life story as she has told it, but also a simple declarative sentence testifying to her greatest achievement: *Dessa rose* above slavery's impediments, transforming herself into a strong, assertive individual with infinite capacity to love, to nurture, and to adapt to changing social conditions, and transforming the world into which she brings the child she and Kaine have conceived into a place where freedom is not a distant dream but an everyday reality. *Dessa rose* to become a woman and a mother in spite of the institution that defined her as an animal and a breeder. Because she could.

NOTES

1. Carole Boyce Davies notes the reversal technique in *Dessa Rose* in her article "Mother Right/Write Revisited: *Beloved* and *Dessa Rose* and the Construction of Motherhood in Black Women's Fiction," in *Narrating Mothers: Theorizing Maternal Subjectivities*, ed. Brenda O. Daly and Maureen T. Reddy (Knoxville: University of Tennessee Press, 1991, 44–57), but fails to explore the implications of this structuring device.

2. In fact, Mary Kemp Davis, in her article entitled "Everybody Knows Her Name: The Recovery of the Past in Sherley Anne Williams's *Dessa Rose*" (*Callaloo* 12:3 [1989]: 544–58), argues that in exercising his power to choose, Kaine assumes a godlike stature, recognizing himself as one of "God's Chosen People" and making Dessa one of the same by "choosing" her for his mate. However, at this point in the narrative, Dessa remains named and directed by a masculine power. Kaine has determined who she is by choosing her; she merely responds. It is only after Kaine's death that Dessa begins to exercise her own power to choose, and thus truly begins the process of actual *self*-determination.

3. See Deborah E. McDowell's article "Negotiating Between Tenses:

Witnessing Slavery after Freedom—*Dessa Rose*" for a more complete discussion of the ways in which Dessa "masters" her own story through her subversive use of language in her conversations with Nehemiah (in *Slavery and the Literary Imagination* [Baltimore, MD: The Johns Hopkins University Press, 1989, 144–63]). Mary Kemp Davis also pays close attention to Dessa's habit of "signifying" in reclaiming and relating her story.

4. It is important to note that Ruth develops such tendencies as the narrative progresses, both as a result of her willing involvement in the blacks' con scheme and through her growing awareness that the slaveholding mentality was ultimately responsible for the corruption of her husband, Bertie.

5. Harrison defines a "post-pastoral" community as one in which "the characters' interaction with the land become secondary to the new community envisioned" (129), a definition that indeed seems appropriate in describing *Dessa Rose*, a novel whose primary concern is interpersonal relationships.

6. It is interesting to note that when Ruth initially mentions this plan, Dessa openly discourages her, obviously still mistrustful and jealous of her. When Ruth introduces the term "friends" into the equation, signalling her acceptance of Dessa and the other blacks as equals, Dessa wants no part of the conversation, still unable to put faith in any relationship other than master-slave between a white person and a black. In the Epilogue, however, Dessa's reminiscences of Ruth and their parting seem tinged with regret: "She couldn't've caused us no more trouble than what the white folks gave us without her. . . . Miss her in and out of trouble—(Do she call my name to Clara?" (259).

7. I should note that here Dessa is guilty of what many whites of her time were guilty of, namely, making an exception of their race prejudices for someone they like. Interestingly, however, she admits that her opinion of Ruth has only "changed *some*" (emphasis mine); Dessa's complete acceptance of Ruth does not occur until their encounter with Nehemiah in the sheriff's office. In fact, I would argue that Dessa's full appreciation of Ruth as a person, and not as a white person, comes only after they have parted permanently. See my remarks later in this chapter.

8. The term is Henri Bergson's (*Comedy* [New York: Doubleday, 1956]). He employs the word to describe "the cheat cheated" and further explains, "the root idea involves an inversion of the roles, and a situation which recoils on the head of its author" (121–22). Deborah McDowell introduces the term in her article "Negotiating Between Tenses: Witnessing Slavery after Freedom—*Dessa Rose*" to discuss the laughter that she argues infuses the novel.

9. Much of the urgency surrounding breast-feeding had to do with the

lack of sanitary conditions—no sterilization procedures and no efficient method of refrigeration—and the subsequent inconvenience associated with bottle-feeding.

10. Ashraf H. A. Rushdy presents an extended interpretation of Ruth's character in his article "Reading Mammy: The Subject of Relation in Sherley Anne Williams' *Dessa Rose*" (*African American Review* 27:3 [1982]: 365–89). Much of his argument centers around his conviction that Ruth's interaction with blacks, beginning with her relationship with Dorcas, is governed by a "repertoire of narratives" (373) she creates about them. This tendency, Rushdy argues, allows her a certain amount of control over their lives, but also results in confusion and misreading on her part.

11. It is important to observe that Ruth has previously engaged in a pattern of denial when it came to the realities of slave existence. Recall, for instance, the fact that although she asked Bertie to refrain from beating their enslaved men and women, she is never completely convinced that he has, in fact, desisted in this method of punishment, and wonders privately whether he has merely moved the beatings out of earshot. The speculation proves to be quite troubling to her, but she never questions Bertie openly about the matter.

12. Nehemiah accumulates a veritable catalogue of animal images in describing Dessa. He refers to her variously as "a wild and timorous animal" (15), a "wildcat" (16), and a "pack animal" (27). He compares her eyes to "a horse's tail flicking him away" (24), calls her a "cow" (31) and a fierce-looking woman "poised on her haunches" (37) waiting to "whelp" (15).

13. The basic premise of Hedin's article is that black fiction writers are overtly conscious of and manipulative of the form their narratives assume as a means of controlling and channeling the pent-up anger their protagonists feel. "Emphasis on form," Hedin argues, "implicitly conveys the rationality of the writer; and that context of rationality allows him to express his anger, or the anger of his characters, without suggesting an overall lack of control" (37). The article appeared before the publication of *Dessa Rose*, but Hedin discusses, among other works, *Imperium in Imperio* (Sutton Griggs, 1899), *Home to Harlem* (Claude McKay, 1928), *Black Thunder* (Arna Bontemps, 1936), *Native Son* (Richard Wright, 1940), *Invisible Man* (Ralph Ellison, 1952), and *The Bluest Eye* (Toni Morrison, 1970).

14. A separate study might be done on Williams' treatment of female stereotypes in *Dessa Rose*. Briefly, Mammy and Jezebel are two stereotypes of black slave women that Deborah Gray White defines and explicates in her book *Ar'n't I a Woman? Female Slaves in the Plantation South*. In the concluding chapter of her work she posits a third stereotype,

Sapphire, and argues that black women living in twentieth-century America have not escaped the categorization that was imposed on their maternal ancestors. It is my contention that Williams depicts Dessa to protest these stereotypes, combining what is good in each of them: Dessa directs Mammy's nurturing impulse towards herself and her own family, coopts Jezebel's wanton sexuality into creative, transformative potential thereby being able to control the terms of her own intimacy, and demonstrates Sapphire's fortitude in overcoming man-made and societal obstacles to freedom, personhood, and motherhood.

3

The Politics of Gender in Toni Morrison's *Beloved*: If "a man ain't nothing but a man," Then What Is a Woman?

Near the beginning of Toni Morrison's *Beloved*, Sethe reflects on Sweet Home, the plantation where she lived as an enslaved woman. What she remembers is its natural beauty, especially its trees. "It shamed her—remembering the wonderful soughing trees rather than the boys . . . hanging from the most beautiful sycamores in the world. . . . Try as she might to make it otherwise, the sycamores beat out the children every time" (6). By the end of the novel, however, Sethe has revised her memory; thinking specifically of the sights she passed on her escape from the plantation she recalls, "pass[ing] right by those boys hanging in the trees. One had Paul A's shirt on but not his feet or his head" (198). The headless, footless body swinging ignobly from the tree is perhaps the last thing that Sethe, pregnant and brutally beaten, sees as she flees Sweet Home to meet up with her children in the North. The return of the memory, and Sethe's subsequent revision of it, signals an acknowledgment of her enslaved past and all its "unspeakable thoughts, unspoken" (199) and her growing willingness to look to the future. The image also stands for something else in the larger context of the novel; it is not only a reminder of the malignancy of slavery in a novel filled with many such reminders, but it also bears witness to the psychological effects of slavery that lingered

long after the institution itself died away. Through *Beloved*, Toni
Morrison has given twentieth-century readers an unparalleled account of American slavery by insisting on the full humanity of
enslaved persons and by demonstrating how two former enslaved
persons can unite the "best thing" (272) in each of them to create
a bona-fide American family, free from physical and spiritual
ghosts.

Morrison's novel has provoked and amazed literary critics; a
virtual industry of *Beloved* (and, by extension, Morrisonian) scholarship has evolved, fueled, in part, by the Pulitzer Prize awarded
to that work in 1988 and, most recently, Morrison's selection in
1993 by the Swedish Academy to receive the Nobel Prize in Literature. Trudier Harris, in an overview of Morrison's career written shortly after the Swedish Academy's announcement, sums up
Morrison's personal achievement in *Beloved*, as well as the novel's
significance to American literature as a whole. "Morrison has written a national epic with a twist, firmly rooting black people in the
polluted American soil of their slave heritage and transforming that
soil to a garden of possibility through the tremendous force of the
human will to survive and to thrive. She has thereby reclaimed
America for the best of itself" ("Toni Morrison" 10).

Scholars who take on the project of reading *Beloved* have fo-
cused largely on issues of motherhood and maternity, looking at
the ways that Morrison has problematized fundamental assumptions about what it means to be a mother and, more precisely, what
motherhood *could* mean during slavery. Stephanie A. Demetrakopoulos, for instance, in her article entitled "Maternal Bonds as
Devourers of Women's Individuation in Toni Morrison's *Beloved*,"
offers a Jungian analysis of the novel. Taking as her subject "the
dark and painful side of mothering, the fact that mothering can
extinguish the developing self of the mother, sometimes even before
that individuation can really begin" (51), she concludes that *Beloved* dramatizes "the death of the maternal" (58) in a woman, in
order that her whole self might be free. Barbara Offutt Mathieson
approaches the novel from a psychoanalytic perspective in "Memory and Mother Love in Morrison's *Beloved*." Tracing the developmental stages a child goes through, Mathieson explicates the
protagonist's psychological scars by noting an affinity between
memory and maternal love, two things that Sethe has an over-

abundance of. "Giving Body to the Word: The Maternal Symbolic in Toni Morrison's *Beloved*" enters the text from a similar angle; here Jean Wyatt applies Lacanian psychoanalytic theory to interpret Morrison's use of language and metaphor, positing an alternative (the maternal symbolic) to the system of master definition, the patriarchal symbolic order.[1]

However, as Deborah Ayer Sitter points out, "the meaning of slavery's impact on a people encompasses more than maternal love; it involves the way internalization of oppressors' values can distort *all* intimate human relationships and even subvert the self" (18, emphasis added). This is precisely Morrison's concern in *Beloved*. She brings to the novel a decidedly womanist perspective, a perspective that allows for, in fact, demands, consideration of all people, not just mothers. The term "womanist," credited to Alice Walker and introduced in *In Search of Our Mothers' Gardens*, resonates with meaning for much of the work being written by African American women in the late twentieth century. Walker defines a person who subscribes to this philosophy as "[c]ommitted to survival and wholeness of [her] entire people, male *and* female" (xi).[2] Morrison has stated that the germ for each novel she writes is a question, and the query that started her thinking about her fifth novel was "Who is the beloved?" For much of the novel, Sethe is unable to recognize the beloved; slavery has denied her wholeness, and the role she has most fully embraced—motherhood—has skewed her perception to such a degree that her idea of protecting her children has become "safety with a handsaw" (164), an image that captures the profound paradox of enslaved motherhood.[3]

Slavery's debilitating impact reached beyond the institution of motherhood though. By denying the possibility of family, slavery not only disrupted the natural maternal bonding process a mother and her child share but denied all blacks, regardless of gender, participation in the most symbolic microcosm of American society. Philip Page argues that "Family—the creation of it, the attempt to preserve it, the nostalgia for it—dominates the plot" (32).[4] It is not merely the absence of the daughter whom she killed rather than see remanded to slavery that haunts Sethe. Her husband is gone, she left behind her extended plantation family when she ran away from the ironically named Sweet Home, and Baby Suggs' community welcomes her only briefly. "The twenty-eight days of

having women friends, a mother-in-law, and all her children together; of being part of a neighborhood; of, in fact, having neighbors at all to call her own—all that was long gone and would never
come back. . . . Those twenty-eight happy days were followed by
eighteen years of disapproval and a solitary life" (173). For Sethe,
freedom means having family and neighbors *of her own* around
her, something easily recognizable as part of the American dream.
Sethe attempts to redefine herself as a participant in this component of the American dream once she is outside the confines of
slavery. However, the American dream did not extend its promise
to enslaved and formerly enslaved persons.

If "definitions belonged to the definers—not the defined" (190),
then post-slavery liberation must have been an amorphous existence at best. The given world that Morrison creates at the beginning of the novel is itself characterized by a lack of definition. The
opening sentence reads, "124 was spiteful" (3). What we eventually learn is the family home is identified only by a number that
relates to no apparent system of organization and by an adjective
ordinarily reserved for humans. The "spite" is described in the next
sentence only as "a baby's venom"; the gender of the child is not
given, nor is the reason for its wrath. The house is a commonplace
gray and white, originally without even the identifying number
"because Cincinnati didn't stretch that far" (3). Like Baby Suggs,
who at the time of the novel's opening is "suspended between the
nastiness of life and the meanness of death" (3–4), readers finds
themselves at the edge of a world at once murky and mysterious,
a world where the shapes of things and their causes are nebulous.
The evocation of such a place surely suggests what life was like
for freed or fugitive enslaved men and women.

Lacking a head, and therefore a face by which to identify it, the
corpse Sethe sees as she leaves Sweet Home is a key to understanding the themes of identity and self-definition with which Morrison
is concerned in *Beloved*. From the opening pages of the novel it is
apparent that conventional gender definitions are blurred; all of
the enslaved persons, not just Paul A, are "faceless," an indication
of what Hortense Spillers identifies as the "gender-neutral" quality
of enslaved existence.[5] In renarrativizing history, Morrison calls
attention to the way she genders her characters in order to dramatize what she perceives as perhaps the cruelest legacy of slavery:

an alienation even from the self. Each of the characters bears some evidence of what I have termed "gender-blurring."[6] This technique manifests itself most dramatically, however, in Paul D and Sethe, the two characters most immediately linked to slavery.[7] While it is not precisely a reversal that occurs, Paul D is endowed with many characteristics that we typically associate with women, while Sethe has assumed a number of "masculine" qualities.

Before examining how Morrison treats gender in the narrative and the consequences of her gendering choices, it is worthwhile to note that this is not the only area obfuscated by blurring in *Beloved*. The slave narrative genre itself is characterized by a blurring between fact and fiction; the narratives of ex-slaves written in the nineteenth century occupy a liminal space somewhere between autobiography, literature, and history.[8] Similarly, Morrison's twentieth-century recreation of the slave narrative is historically imaginative and imaginatively historical. Also, Jean Wyatt notes that what she perceives as the central relationship in *Beloved*, that between Sethe and Beloved, is characterized by a natural blurring that necessarily occurs between any mother and her infant.

The dedifferentiation of the possessive pronouns [throughout the narrative, but especially in the three monologues at the center of the narrative] dramatizes the impossibility of separating what belongs to the one body from what belongs to the other when the two are joined by the nipple or, rather, by the milk that flows between them, blurring borders. . . . Nursing serves as a figure for the totality and exclusivity of mother-daughter fusion. (481)

These examples serve to draw attention to blurring as a fundamental component of the narrative strategy Morrison utilizes to reinvigorate the slave narrative genre. However, the manner with which she treats gender is a topic that has received considerably less attention; it is my contention that gender-blurring is crucial to an understanding of Morrison's explication of slavery, personhood, family, and identity.

The first clue to Morrison's unusual approach to gendering her characters comes in the first paragraph of the novel. We are told that "the sons, Howard and Buglar, had run away" (3), victims of the "baby's venom" that infects the house. Their decision to run is clearly contrasted with the behavior of their grandmother, Baby Suggs, their mother, Sethe, and their sister, Denver, all of whom stay in the family home and cope with the unusual incidents they attribute to a child's ghost. As a result, the boys are defined in terms of behavior that is decidedly unmanly; instead of confronting their fears, they opt for running from them. And theirs is not the usual male desire to roam, a recurrent trope in African American literature, but rather a flight motivated solely by fright. What remains is a community of women bound together by their determination to live as ordinary an existence as possible under circumstances as extraordinary as having as a houseguest a ghost who leaves baby handprints in a cake.

In fact, it is Paul D and not the ghost who is the intrusive presence in the house; his arrival upsets what has become routine existence at 124. His response to what he perceives to be an evil spirit in Sethe's home may be read as typically male—he confronts, and when he is not satisfied, he resorts to violent action.

"God damn it! Hush up!" Paul D was shouting, falling, reaching for anchor. "Leave the place alone! Get the hell out!" A table rushed toward him and he grabbed its leg. Somehow he managed to stand at an angle and, holding the table by two legs, he bashed it about, wrecking everything, screaming back at the screaming house. "You want to fight, come on! God damn it! She got enough without you. She got enough!" (18)

While it is important not to be essentialist in ascribing certain reactions exclusively to males and others to females, it is generally held that men more often than women choose aggressive, confrontational behavior, particularly when they feel threatened or bested. Trudier Harris, in her book *Fiction and Folklore: The Novels of Toni Morrison*, notes that 124 immediately poses a threat to Paul D, and she identifies the nature of the threat as overtly female. "Paul D's arrival at Sethe's house brings with it the ancient fear of women. When he enters the house haunted by Beloved's ghost, it becomes the enveloping enclosure of the vagina; the vagina dentata myth operates as Paul D *feels* the physical threat of the house. . . . He perceives that it bodes no good for him, and he senses—more than he knows—that the contest is between male and female spirits" (155). Perceiving a need to assert (and perhaps confirm) his masculinity, he chooses to exercise his will, and for a time it seems as if he is successful—the house and its ghost are quiet, submissive.

Fighting as an expression of manhood is also played out in the character of Mr. Garner, the white man who owns Sweet Home and its slaves until the time of his death. Garner is unusual in that he endeavors to treat the enslaved persons on his plantation as human beings, asking for and respecting their opinions, refusing to beat them, and even allowing one of them, Halle, to purchase his mother's freedom. However, it is important to acknowledge that Garner still considers himself superior to his enslaved men, because he can choose to and afford to be generous to lesser men. Aggression, the question of manhood, and the institution of slavery merge in a recurring incident in which Garner takes inordinate pride.

> "Y'all got boys," he told them. "Young boys, old boys, picky boys, stropping boys. Now at Sweet Home, my niggers is men every one of em. Bought em thataway, raised em thataway. Men every one."
> "Beg to differ, Garner. Ain't no nigger men."
> "Not if you scared, they ain't." Garner's smile was wide. "But if you a man yourself, you'll want your niggers to be men too."
> "I wouldn't have no nigger men round my wife."
> It was the reaction Garner loved and waited for. "Neither would I," he said. "Neither would I," and there was always a pause before the neighbor, or stranger, or peddler, or brother-in-law or whoever it was got the meaning. Then a fierce argument, sometimes a fight, and Garner came home bruised and pleased, having demonstrated one more time what a real Kentuckian was: one tough enough and smart enough to make and call his own niggers men. (10–11)

Garner's quest to prove his manhood here is apparent, and Paul D's actions in Sethe's kitchen are no different from Garner's instigation of his fellow slaveholders. In both cases manhood is asserted through aggression and violent behavior.

Garner's benevolent treatment of the men and women he owned is problematized along the very lines of gender, however. His generous attitude blatantly contradicts the fundamental assumption of slavery: that enslaved men and women are property rather than persons. As Angela Davis points out in *Women, Race and Class*, "The slave system defined Black people as chattel. Since women, no less than men, were viewed as profitable labor-units, [both] might as well have been genderless as far as the slaveholders were concerned" (5). In other words, the gender of an enslaved African simply did not matter, unless that person was a woman about to give birth. Thus by coupling the dehumanizing rigors inherent in a life of slavery with humane gestures towards their personhood, Garner heightens the confusion the men and women he owned surely must have felt by the very fact of their enslaved condition. Paul D reflects this confusion when he meditates on the feelings he experiences while being watched by "Mister," the rooster at Sweet Home with the all-too-human name.

"He sat right there on the tub looking at me. I swear he smiled. My head was full of what I'd seen of Halle a while back. I wasn't even thinking about the bit. Just Halle and before him Sixo, but when I saw Mister I knew it was me too. Not just them, me too. One crazy, one sold, one missing, one burnt and me licking iron with my hands crossed behind me. The last of the Sweet Home men . . . Mister, he looked so . . . free. Better than me. Stronger, tougher . . . Mister was allowed to be and stay what he was. But I wasn't allowed to be and stay what I was. Even if you cooked him you'd be cooking a rooster named Mister. But wasn't no way I'd ever be Paul D again, living or dead." (72)

Harris argues that Mister is "an objectification of freedom and a metaphor for manhood . . . more 'man' than Paul D, more human—in the sense of having a separate, individual identity—than human beings who are slaves" (*Fiction* 181). Many years after his escape from slavery, Paul D still feels less than fully a man, tormented by the memory of a rooster infinitely more free than himself, a fact that further problematizes Garner's seemingly benevolent intentions.

Paul D recognizes that it is the institution of slavery, and Garner's peculiar interpretation of it, that has shaped his identity. As he grows older, however, "he wondered how much difference there really was between before schoolteacher and after. Garner called and announced them men—but only on Sweet Home, and by his leave. Was he naming what he saw or creating what he did not? . . . What would he have been anyway—before Sweet Home— without Garner?" (220). The issue of his manhood plagues Paul

D to the extent that he asks Sethe to have his child, an age-old way of proving manhood.[9] But what is clearly more at stake in the course of Paul D's troubling thoughts is the issue of personhood. He wonders who he is and how he has come to be who he is. For as long as Garner is alive he is a "man," but after Garner's death he is something else, defined in a different way by a different definer. With Garner's death and the subsequent abuse received at schoolteacher's hands, Paul D becomes a different person; the Paul D who arrives on Sethe's doorstep eighteen years after her flight from Sweet Home has a "tobacco tin" (113) in the place where his heart should be. However, he also has a number of feminine qualities, acquired in the process of trying to forge an integrated identity for himself outside the bonds of slavery. It is in looking at some of Paul D's "feminine" attributes, and in paralleling them with Sethe's defining characteristics, that the significance of Morrison's intentional gender-blurring becomes apparent.

According to Mary Field Belenky and her fellow researchers who in the late 1970s conducted an extensive interview-based study in an attempt to categorize the differing ways "women view reality and draw conclusions about truth, knowledge, and authority" (3), there are patterns of knowing that can be characterized as "female" and such gender-specific traits manifest themselves in direct relation to life experience and circumstance. The authors of this study, eventually published in book form as *Women's Ways of Knowing: The Development of Self, Voice, and Mind*, group the ways women come to know themselves and the world around them into five epistemological categories—silence, received knowledge, subjective knowledge, procedural knowledge, and constructural knowledge— but are careful to acknowledge that these are fluid, not fixed, categories, and that similar categories can be found in men's thinking (15). They stress the developmental aspect of epistemology, pointing out that many individuals reach a particular stage of awareness or type of knowing but do not progress beyond it. Furthermore, they very early identify several salient characteristics of women's speech that are crucial to understanding their subsequent classifications: the authors, citing a number of sociolinguistic studies, posit a style for women that may be classified as "hesitant, qualified, question-posing" and content that normally is "concern[ed] for the everyday, the practical, and the interpersonal"; the authors

further point out that this manner of speaking is "typically deval-
ued by men and women alike" (17). Their interviews with hundreds of women from a variety of backgrounds, conducted over a
five-year period, are an attempt at understanding precisely why it
is women perceive and react in speech the way they do.

Nancy Chodorow, too, refers to a "core gender identity" that is
established in childhood and distinguishes between male and female. "What we develop at such an early stage is a general rela-
tional stance: girls see themselves in relation to their mothers and
as connected to the world; boys see themselves as separate from
and in opposition to their mothers and as separate from the world"
(Spelman 96). According to both of these definitions,[10] Paul D sees
and responds to the world in a way that is far more characteristic
of a woman than of a man. The hallmarks of his thought and
action are intuitiveness and connectedness. For example, his uneasy
reaction to the arrival of Beloved is based on intuition; when Sethe
asks him what bothers him about her he replies, "I can't place it.
It's a feeling in me" (67). He feels an affinity with others very
keenly, whether it is a literal connectedness, as when he is part of
the coffle in Alfred, Georgia, or a spiritual bond like that he experiences when he looks upon Sethe's back for the first time.

Behind her, bending down, his body an arc of kindness, he held her breasts
in the palms of his hands. He rubbed his cheek on her back and learned
that way her sorrow, the roots of it; its wide trunk and intricate branches.
Raising his fingers to the hooks of her dress, he knew without seeing them
or hearing any sigh that the tears were coming fast. And when the top of
her dress was around her hips and he saw the sculpture her back had
become, like the decorative work of an ironsmith too passionate for display, he could think but not say, "Aw, Lord, girl." And he would tolerate
no peace until he had touched every ridge and leaf of it with his mouth,
none of which Sethe could feel because her back skin had been dead for
years. (17–18)

Here we witness Paul D "learning" Sethe's story intuitively, as opposed to rationally and scientifically, characteristically male ways
of knowing. His hands take the place of his other senses and he
"feels" in both meanings of the word, becoming moved beyond
language when he experiences the horror that Sethe has endured.

His connectedness with her and her story is one that occurs outside the boundaries of language; it is one of pure emotion.

Prior to his touching Sethe and learning her story, Paul D gives another hint as to the type of man he is. Although I have noted that he does on occasion manifest typically "male" behavior[11] and he himself confesses, "Men don't know nothing much" (16), he stands apart from other men in being able to recognize deep emotion. Walking into 124 and "straight into a pool of red and undulating light that locked him where he stood" (8), Paul D instinctively realizes that Sethe bears an overwhelming sorrow, a sorrow that he immediately shares. He does not, as other men might, shy away from the emotion he feels; instead he allows it to embrace him, and thus furthers the newly forged connection he has with Sethe. "Walking through it, a wave of grief soaked him so thoroughly he wanted to cry . . . the grief had soaked him. The red was gone but a kind of weeping clung to the air where it had been" (9–10). We cannot miss the narrative emphasis that Morrison places.

It is this capacity for empathy that enables Paul D to share in a sort of "sisterhood" with women. We are told that:

Not even trying, he had become the kind of man who could walk into a house and make the women cry. Because with him, in his presence, they could. There was something blessed in his manner. Women saw him and wanted to weep—to tell him that their chest hurt and their knees did too. Strong women and wise saw him and told him things they only told each other: that way past the Change of Life, desire in them had suddenly become enormous, greedy, more savage than when they were fifteen, and that it embarrassed them and made them sad; that secretly they longed to die—to be quit of it—that sleep was more precious to them than any waking day. Young girls sidled up to him to confess or describe how well-dressed the visitations were that had followed them straight from their dreams. (17)

Paul D can make women cry, but it is not "macho" or righteously masculine behavior that causes their tears; rather, it is his gentle manner that fosters their openness. The very nature of the confidences women share with him is testimony to the power of his feminine attributes. Listening and feeling places Paul D on the "received knower" rung of the Belenky hierarchy of learning, a step that enables him to bridge the self-other gap effectively.

Morrison's revision of history is perhaps even more apparent in the way she genders Sethe's character. Karla C. Holloway argues that Morrison dramatizes "a history of absence because slavery denied them [black women] the right to nurture, the physical and psychic assurance of generation, and a promise of cultural and generational continuity" (169). Two contrasting images serve to delineate Sethe's character, working together to create the same sort of gender-blurring that we have seen in the depiction of Paul D.

Jean Wyatt argues that in depicting Sethe, Morrison is "elaborating the figure of the heroic slave mother that in many female slave narratives replaces the figure of the heroic male fugitive" (475), but yet differentiates her heroine from women like Harriet Jacobs and Lucy Delaney by insisting on the *literal* ability to nurture that her enslaved mother possesses: "Sethe's monumental body and abundant milk give and sustain life" (476).[12] Indeed, that Sethe has typically female qualities is unmistakable; she is, after all, defined almost exclusively as a mother, identified repeatedly by the milk that flows from her breasts: "Milk was all I ever had" (159).

Perhaps nowhere do we see more clearly the commodification of the body in slavery than in the instance of Sethe's milk, which rightfully belongs to her children, but which is forcibly taken from her by schoolteacher's nephews while he watches and records in his book. This incident is by no means an aberration; it is well documented that enslaved women were highly prized as long as they were able to be "breeders," and the abundant breasts of a nursing mother, source of misery for the woman herself, were nevertheless an apt reminder of her fecundity. Moses Grandy reported, "On the estate I am speaking of, those women who had sucking children suffered much from their breasts becoming full of milk, the infants being left at home. They therefore could not keep up with the other hands; I have seen the overseer beat them with raw hide, so that the blood and milk flew mingled from their breasts" (Davis and Gates 9). Morrison recreates a similar scene at the time of the infanticide; we are told that "Denver took her mother's milk right along with the blood of her sister" (152). At every turn we

are reminded of Sethe's nurturing properties; the repeated references to her breasts emphasize both the womanly dignity of her
desire to feed the child she has spirited away and the inhuman
indignity she has suffered at the hands of the white slaveholders.
Along these same lines it is important to note that after escaping
from Sweet Home, Sethe enjoys precisely "twenty-eight days—the
travel of one whole moon—of unslaved life" (95), clearly an al-
lusion to the course of a woman's menstrual cycle. Morrison perhaps suggests that it is only when completely outside the
boundaries of slavery that a woman can truly *be* a woman. The
infanticide and its consequences, seen in this light, represent merely
another form of slavery for Sethe; though she remains a free
woman after her prison term, she becomes an all-too-literal slave
to the past. It is at this point that many of her masculine traits
surface.[13]

The second image associated with Sethe in the text is a warlike
one, and it recurs with startling frequency. Remembering Baby
Suggs' voice, Sethe hears, " 'Lay em down, Sethe. Sword and
shield. Down. Down. Both of them down. Down by the riverside.
Sword and shield. Don't study war no more. Lay all that mess
down. Sword and shield.' And under the pressing fingers and the
quiet instructive voice, she would. Her heavy knives of defense
against misery, regret, gall, and hurt, she placed one by one on a
bank where clear water rushed on below" (86). Sethe has acquired
an arsenal of defenses against the past; in her own words, "The
future was a matter of keeping the past at bay" (42). And although
Sethe takes Baby Suggs' advice periodically and lets down her defenses, for most of the eighteen years she conducts active warfare,
a decidedly male activity, against the past and its occurrences. She
is indeed militant in the protection of her children, and in the protection of her emotions as well. When Paul D arrives at 124 and
begins caressing her back, she is tempted to put "the responsibility
for her breasts . . . in somebody else's hands" (18), but by the next
morning she has reappraised the situation; although she makes it
clear that Paul D is welcome to stay, she persists in her isolation.[14]

Sethe's isolation from the strong female-centered community is
obvious as well; her pronounced estrangement from her community is indicative of the degree of her isolation,[15] and illustrates the
idea of gender-blurring as well. The women do not embrace her,

it is true; many view her as more a monster than a woman, wondering what woman could be capable of killing her own child.[16] But Sethe also does not seek community, for reasons of pride (a quality the town women make much of, perhaps to justify their avoidance of her), shame, and the chore of keeping the past at arm's length. What results is further emphasis on her role at home, her role as a woman who believes that her children are her "best thing"—a concept that Paul D dismisses as motherlove "too thick" (164).

Images of milk, blood, and war cooperate in portraying Sethe as possessing traits typical of both genders, a fact that is further indicated by her name. She remembers that her mother, who had borne several children but only kept Sethe, named her for the black man who was her father; thus she carries a man's name through life, although perhaps we may read the "e" on Seth as an attempt to feminize the name. Furthermore, when Sethe meets Amy in the woods, she does not tell the white girl her real name, but identifies herself as "Lu," a name that may be heard as male as well as female.

Sethe has not progressed as far on Belenky's hierarchy of ways of knowing as has Paul D. For the bulk of the narrative she sees the self largely through the eyes of others—first, those "others" who have the power to define her, and then those who see her only through the veil of the defining act that she commits. If attempts at self-definition arise from concrete social and occupational roles as Belenky et al. suggest (50), then it is little wonder that Sethe leads a life of isolation and alienation. For in her post-slavery existence she is defined chiefly by means of her role as mother, and she has violated the implicit rules of this contract in the worst possible way. But Sethe's condition stems not so much from the act she commits after her escape from slavery as from the general circumstances surrounding the life of a slave.

Belenky et al. emphasize that a connective, intuitive approach to the world is shaped as a result of "maternal authority" (62), something that Sethe lacks almost completely. As a child she sees her mother very rarely, and only when she is pointed out to her in the field.

Of that place where she was born . . . she remembered only song and dance. Not even her own mother, who was pointed out to her by the

eight-year-old child who watched over the young ones—pointed out as
the one among many backs turned away from her, stooping in a watery
field. Patiently Sethe waited for this particular back to gain the row's end
and stand. What she saw was a cloth hat as opposed to a straw one,
singularity enough in that world of cooing women each of whom was
called Ma'am. (30)

The reader cannot miss the generic quality of motherhood as it
is illustrated in this passage; slavewomen give birth only for the
sake of increasing the labor force, and an intimate relationship
with their children has no place in the process. Sethe's mother is
merely a "back" that wears a cloth hat; later she identifies herself
to the young Sethe by means of the brand that she bears under-
neath her breast.[17] This is the extent of Sethe's knowledge of her
personal history.

That she seeks a female role model is evident, however, and it
is both poignant and ironic that she turns to Mrs. Garner at the
time of her marriage, asking her, "Is there a wedding?" (26), and
knowing that a bride wore a special dress and had a celebratory
feast only because she has seen Mrs. Garner's dress in storage and
heard stories about the elaborate preparations for the wedding
meal (59). Later, Baby Suggs provides some of the awareness that
Sethe seeks, aiding her in the care of the children when she finally
arrives at 124, something Sethe knows virtually nothing about because "[w]asn't nobody to ask. Mrs. Garner never had no children
and we was the only women there" (159). But the gap that Sethe
experiences is profound; she feels typical maternal urges but is unsure how to go about fulfilling them and, ultimately, how to construct a meaningful existence for herself outside of slavery.

As a result of her lack of formative experiences in slavery and
the terrible deed that she commits knowingly, Sethe adopts a pattern of consciously "walking away from the past" (Belenky et al.
77). The story of *Beloved* becomes, then, Sethe's painful reac-
quaintance with the past. It is a difficult process; as Amy Denver,
the white girl who assists Sethe in her escape, points out as she
massages Sethe's bruised and swollen feet, "Anything dead coming
back to life hurts" (35). With the introduction first of Paul D and
then of Beloved, Sethe gradually sheds her isolationist pose and,
when the fateful moment recurs in the yard of 124, she is able both
to accept the embrace of the community of women who have gath-

ered and to direct her vengeance at an "other" (Mr. Bodwin) rather than at her own "best thing." Furthermore, after the reenactment of the infanticide during which she mistakes Mr. Bodwin in his cart for schoolteacher and his hat come for her children, Sethe is finally ready to listen as Paul D instructs:

"You your best thing, Sethe. You are."
. . .
"Me? Me?" (273)

Mae G. Henderson, in an article entitled "Toni Morrison's *Beloved*: Re-Membering the Body as Historical Text," argues that in her effort to deal with her past, "Sethe, in effect, creates a counternarrative that reconstitutes her humanity and demonstrates the requirements of motherlove. . . . A story of oppression becomes a story of liberation; a story of inhumanity has been overwritten as a story of higher humanity" (79–80). In affirming, albeit in question form, that she is her own "best thing," Sethe finally claims for herself an identity all her own, completing the process she began with her response to Bodwin. Her action in the yard demonstrates a newfound response to intuition and feeling as she allows the past to surface so that she can come to terms with it, legitimize it, and relegate it to where it ultimately belongs—the past. In the concluding episodes of the narrative it becomes apparent that Morrison privileges women's ways of knowing, emphasizing connectedness, feeling and emotion, intuition—and that these things are, in fact, consonant with motherlove.

Paul D's perception is keen when he recognizes the danger both of Sethe's attachment to her children and of what Henderson terms Sethe's "counternarrative." "Risky, thought Paul D, very risky. For a used-to-be-slave woman to love anything that much was dangerous, especially if it was her children she had settled on to love. The best thing, he knew, was to love just a little bit; everything, just a little bit, so when they broke its back, or shoved it in a croaker sack, well, maybe you'd have a little love left over for the next one" (45). The end result of slavery, both the condition of enslaved existence and the legacy of the institution itself, is the defamiliarization of the person, an estrangement both from one's body (Sethe's reproductive rights and her milk are not her own but are appropriated by the white master) and from one's emotions (motherlove becomes a danger). This may be directly traced to the commodification of the body. A body owned by another is a different body, and this returns us to the question of gender and self-definition in the novel. It is not uncommon to read a novel in which characters share traits of both genders, and it has not been my intention to establish that *Beloved* is merely another such novel. Rather, it is interesting to note that it occurs, but also to observe the ways in which Morrison prioritizes "women's ways of knowing" (to use Belenky's phrase again) precisely by attributing them mostly to a male character, and by dramatizing the female character's struggle to know and accept the past in a healthy way, a way that reveals itself, finally, as feminine.

Portraits of strong women have become somewhat of a tradition in Morrison's fiction, and it is my contention that there is a precedent for gender-blurring in her work before the neo-slave narrative *Beloved*. The young heroine of Morrison's 1973 novel *Sula* cuts off part of her finger to prove her toughness to neighborhood bullies who have made it their practice to harrass her and Nel as they walk home from school. This gesture is typically "male" in its spirit of aggression and confrontation. Furthermore, Sula takes as her motto the belief that "there was no other [than the self] you could count on" (118–19), a personal philosophy that succeeds in alienating her from the entire Bottom community. Sexual intercourse is, for Sula, a time to "feel . . . her own abiding strength and limitless power" (123), and the mutual attraction she and Ajax share is based largely on "his refusal to baby or protect her" (128); their relationship ends only when Sula begins to feel a deeper emotional attachment to Ajax and becomes overly domestic in her possessiveness, a seeming contradiction in her character that Morrison either chooses to overlook or chooses simply not to address. Sula is college-educated, rootless, and a committed wanderer and philanderer, more concerned with her own precarious identity than with typical womanly desires to settle down and bear children: "I don't want to make somebody else. I want to make myself" (92). Discussing Morrison's *Sula*, Marianne Hirsch argues in "Maternal Narratives: 'Cruel Enough to Stop the Blood' " that "Sula's rejection of maternity means an assumption of male freedom" (424). Most interesting to this discussion, perhaps, is a comment Sula

makes to Nel near the end of the novel. Nel accuses her of arro-
gance, saying, "You *can't* do it all. You a woman and a colored
woman at that. You can't act like a man. You can't be walking
around all independent-like, doing whatever you like, taking what
you want, leaving what you don't." Sula replies, "I'm a woman
and colored. Ain't that the same as being a man?" (142) Morrison
tantalizes the reader with this assertion but fails to explore fully
the implications of Sula's enigmatic gender-blurring statement.[18]

More positively cast than Sula is Pilate, the dominant female
figure in *Song of Solomon* (1977). The conventional feminine traits
she bears are obvious: she is a mother and a grandmother, a nurturer, a conjurer, a practitioner of folk ways, a storyteller; she
makes wine and teaches Milkman how to cook a perfect soft-
boiled egg. However, she bears a man's name, dresses in men's
clothing, nourishes her family by providing "[w]hatever they had
a taste for" (29), and is clearly the head-of-household in all re-
spects. Joseph T. Skerrett, Jr. asserts that Pilate's "personal power
goes beyond the conventions of her gender" (198). Pilate is linked
to Sethe as well as to Sula by the fact that she does not belong to
any community other than the close circle of her immediate family,
daughter and granddaughter. In fact, although Pilate is the chief
representative of love in the novel, she is isolated from mainstream
society, ostracized by a physiological mark, the fact that she has
no navel.

Morrison herself has identified Pilate as sharing characteristics
of both genders, saying that she is "the best of that which is female
and the best of that which is male, and that balance is disturbed
if it is not nurtured, and if it is not counted on and if it is not
reproduced" (Evans 344). I agree that Pilate is a healthy, well-
balanced figure who does, indeed, possess strong feminine and
masculine traits; however, I would argue that the balance is disturbed in the overall world of the novel. Pilate exists completely
in a woman-centered environment; the world she fosters for her
daughter and her granddaughter has no male role models in it, and
Reba and Hagar do not benefit from the "balanced" perspective
Pilate herself has assimilated when they interact in the "real
world." The consequences are devastating for Hagar.

Neither Pilate nor Reba knew that Hagar was not like them. Not strong
enough, like Pilate, nor simple enough, like Reba, to make up her life as

they had. She needed what most colored girls needed: a chorus of mamas, grandmamas, aunts, cousins, sisters, neighbors, Sunday school teachers, best girl friends, and what all to give her the strength life demanded of her—and the humor with which to live it. (311)

The strong female-centered community Pilate has shaped at the wine house out of her own isolation is insufficient to nurture Hagar; in depicting Pilate, Morrison has created a strong woman who is able to overcome her ostracization, but whose nurturing properties are unconventional; what she passes on to her offspring is not necessarily productive for their existence. Indeed, Morrison—perhaps making a sociological comment on the state of black family life in twentieth-century America—comments that "That is the disability we must be on guard against for the future—the female who reproduces the female who reproduces the female" ("Rootedness" 344).

I contend that Morrison consciously revises herself by duplicating the trio of women in *Song of Solomon* and the implications of their lifestyle in her depiction of the female-headed family in *Beloved*: initially Baby Suggs, Sethe, and Denver, and then Sethe, Denver, and Beloved. Susan Jaret McKinstry characterizes the community the women share as "excessive, oppressive, possessive" (270).[19] This interpretation leads me to my final example of blurring in the novel and to my conclusions about Morrison's valuation of black family life. The first "word" of the novel is not, in fact, a word at all; it is a number, 124. What is missing—what we might argue is "blurred" from the very beginning of the work—is the "3," the anticipated completion of a sequence of three numbers beginning with 1 and 2. The number three is the basis of Western folk, religious, and cultural traditions and has several connotations that we cannot overlook in the context of this novel: it is a number associated with magic, it is laden with Christian symbolism (the Trinity), and it is a number suggestive of the completion of the Western family: father, mother, child.

In the world Morrison imagines in *Beloved*, the integrated self finds its best and fullest expression as a member of a nuclear family, something denied to most enslaved persons. Contemplating her present life—estranged from the community, with only Denver for company—versus "that other one" (42)—her life as an enslaved woman, Sethe must factor another possibility into the equation when Paul D steps into her kitchen. "The fact that Paul D had come out of 'that other one' into her bed was better too; and the notion of a future with him, or for that matter without him, was beginning to stroke her mind" (42). The temptation that Paul D presents *is* the future—the living future, living the future—something only attainable if Sethe can effectively integrate the self she has been at odds with since slavery. In some ways, Paul D is an "ancestor" in this novel, much as Pilate is an ancestral presence in *Song of Solomon*.[20] Morrison says of her work, "There is always an ancestor there. And these ancestors are not just parents, they are sort of timeless people whose relationships to the characters are benevolent, instructive, and protective, and they provide a certain kind of wisdom" ("Rootedness" 343). When Paul D returns he offers the same balance that characterizes Pilate to Sethe and to her household, thus closing the "gap" in Sethe's self and the gap in "124" by providing a sense of the past, the possibility of family, and hope for the future, and by forging a way for the three to coexist meaningfully and peacefully at 124 Bluestone Road.

Meaningful and peaceful coexistence within a family can only occur when all members of the family unit recognize and exercise their full humanity. Angela Davis, in her chapter entitled "The Legacy of Slavery: Standards for a New Womanhood" from *Women, Race and Class*, notes that "men, women, and children alike were all 'providers' for the slaveholding class" (8), and documents accounts of men and women working the same hours and the same tasks and subject to the same beatings. She makes a good case for the "genderlessness" of slavery, suggesting that the institution was responsible for confusion in shaping gender identity, particularly in enslaved women. "Required by the master's demands to be as 'masculine' in the performance of their work as their men, Black women must have been profoundly affected by their experiences during slavery" (11). In "What the Black Woman Thinks About Women's Lib," Morrison herself casts the dilemma enslaved women faced in a more positive light, arguing that the black woman "had nothing to fall back on: not maleness, not whiteness, not ladyhood, not anything. And out of the profound isolation of her reality she may very well have invented herself" (63). But in *Beloved* she complicates this assertion, demonstrating that self-definition entails more than merely "inventing" the self in the new context of freedom. Whereas Paul D arrived at self-definition by recognizing that he was not just the "man" of Garner's definition but also had feminine traits, traits that enhanced the way in which he related to the world and its individuals,[21] Sethe had to integrate the two sides of her personality, a significantly different task. It is only with the arrival of Paul D, the "ancestor" who looks in no direction other than towards the future, that Sethe is able to resurrect her fully human self. When asked in an interview whether she believes in upward mobility for black people, Morrison responded, "Of course. Absolutely. But I'm not going to give up one drop of melanin in order to get there. I'm not going to erase my race or my gender to get there. I want all of it; I deserve all of it. And we all do. I don't want to be blanded, bleached out in order to participate in this country."[22] What is interesting to note in her response is the fact that although she had been asked about *black* people's progress, Morrison answers in terms of both race and gender. In the Morrisonian scheme of things, a person cannot be fully human if either is denied.

Gender-blurring becomes for Morrison one of the most effective, and poignant, ways to demonstrate the inhumanity of slavery; she dramatizes certain fundamental irrelevancies of gender by bringing together Sethe and Paul D and by blurring the gender characteristics that define them. The world she depicts is, initially, a decentered one, one in which gender identity is indeed a luxury. Perhaps the most moving passage in the novel occurs when Sethe overhears schoolteacher instructing his nephews how to chart Sethe's qualities: " 'No, no. That's not the way. I told you to put her human characteristics on the left; her animal ones on the right. And don't forget to line them up' " (193). To the slaveowner, Sethe is a piece of property, a hybrid of characteristics, some of which belong to a human, others of which define a work animal. This effacement of her personhood directly links her with the corpse she sees hanging from the tree when she leaves Sweet Home and which is her legacy as an enslaved person—she cannot find a way to use it to define herself once she is outside of slavery, and she cannot run from it.

Instead she almost succumbs, allowing Beloved to take over her home and, it seems, her very life. But when Paul D returns to 124, "his coming . . . the reverse route of his going" (263), they are able to complete each other. Paul D, a "walking" man, finds in Sethe the soulmate he has never had, and for whom he recognizes he is finally ready. As the present tense indicates, it is a sudden awareness: "Suddenly he remembers Sixo trying to describe what he felt about the Thirty-Mile Woman. 'She is a friend of my mind. She gather me, man. The pieces I am, she gather them and give them back to me in all the right order' " (272–73). Once Paul D has accepted his condition of fragmentation, a logical consequence of a life of enslavement (whether to another person or to the past), he can free Sethe from her own enslavement, promising her a future in which she is her own "best thing."

> "Sethe," he says, "me and you, we got more yesterday than anybody. We need some kind of tomorrow."
> He leans over and takes her hand. With the other he touches her face. "You your best thing, Sethe. You are." His holding fingers are holding hers. (273)

Sethe's awareness of Paul D's direct touch on her face and his use of her name, both markers of an identity he recognizes, and her perception of his "holding" fingers "holding" hers (which seems to suggest a sort of eternally present moment) individuate her, erasing the effacement she has suffered as a result of slavery. Joined, they are one, able together to face the future, because the past for each of them has been put to rest by the other. The final word of the novel—"Beloved"—serves, I think, not to remind us of the ghost[23] but rather as the term of endearment describing the family that Sethe and Paul D have finally found in each other. It may also be the injunction with which Morrison wishes to leave us: be loved. By renarrativizing history, choosing to dramatize an effect of slavery little recognized, Morrison accomplishes, by the end of the novel, precisely that which she sought to expose: she "genders" her characters by tracing their growth from imposed "genderlessness" to a new order of personhood—shared personhood in which each participant can both love and be loved.

NOTES

Portions of this chapter originally appeared in *Obsidian II: Black Literature in Review* 8:1 (Spring/Summer 1993), reprinted courtesy of *Obsidian II*.

1. Wyatt's article is the most thorough examination of *Beloved* that I have encountered. The thoroughness of her notes and bibliography and her thoughtful, well-grounded insights should prove useful to scholars approaching the text from many angles.

2. For a more complete definition of the term, see Alice Walker's *In Search of Our Mothers' Gardens* (New York: Harcourt Brace Jovanovich, 1983), xi–xii.

3. Morrison discusses the "morality" of Sethe's action in a *New York Times* interview (August 26, 1987, C17) with Mervyn Rothstein. In part she says, "It was absolutely the right thing to do, . . . but it's also the thing you have no right to do." This remark is often quoted and, in fact, has entered into what may be considered the "lore" of *Beloved* scholarship, but the statement is perhaps too coy on Morrison's part.

4. Paul D's arrival extends to Sethe the only promise of family she has had since Baby Suggs' death and her boys' flight. However, it is important to note that initially Paul D and Sethe rekindle the friendship they had developed at Sweet Home; only later in the narrative does Morrison develop the familial ties they share, first by emphasizing the ways Paul D acts like a brother to Sethe and then by according him a more significant role in Sethe's life as her life's partner or soulmate.

5. Unpublished talk, The University of North Carolina at Chapel Hill, Chapel Hill, NC, February 18, 1992.

6. Arguments might also be made for Morrison's use of gender-blurring in depicting Amy Denver, who is characterized by her adventurousness; Baby Suggs, whose great leadership skills are highlighted; and even Denver at the close of the novel, who takes on the responsibility of providing for her family when she conquers her "feminine" fear and walks off the porch at 124 Bluestone.

7. Stephanie A. Demetrakopoulos briefly acknowledges what I have termed "gender-blurring" by applying the Jungian terms "animus" and "anima" to Sethe and Paul D. Demetrakopoulos argues that "Paul D gives Sethe the animus quality of initiative to escape from the mother/family matrix into individuation. . . . Sethe helps Paul D develop his anima qualities of relatedness that make a man responsible to his family and community, that permit him to achieve intimacy and enduring relationships" (57). Demetrakopoulos' conclusions are biased to support her thesis that Morrison's primary intent is to dramatize Sethe's "individuation." As my reading will show, I dispute her contention that these characters "give" these qualities to each other.

8. *The Slave's Narrative*, a collection of essays edited by Charles T. Davis and Henry Louis Gates, Jr., is a good starting point for further discussion of the slave narrative as autobiography/literature/history. See,

especially, Robert B. Stepto's essay "I Rose and Found My Voice: Narration, Authentication, and Authorial Control in Four Slave Narratives" and James Olney's " 'I Was Born': Slave Narratives, Their Status as Autobiography and as Literature" (New York: Oxford University Press, 1985).

9. For a thorough discussion of Paul D's manhood, see Deborah Ayer Sitter's article "The Making of a Man: Dialogic Meaning in *Beloved*" (*African American Review* 26:1 [Spring 1992]: 17–29). Sitter approaches the novel from a new angle; she argues that scholars have overlooked discussions of masculinity and manhood in *Beloved* and that "the meaning of Sethe's story cannot be fully understood except in relation to his [Paul D's]" (17).

10. One additional source that further explores issues of gender development and identity is Carol Gilligan's *In a Different Voice: Psychological Theory and Women's Development* (Cambridge: Harvard University Press, 1982).

11. Undoubtedly such behavior manifests itself as a result of the mixed signals he has received as a slave about how a man should act and respond. The most glaring example in the novel occurs when Paul D confronts the ghost in Sethe's home for the first time, fully unleashing what society would consider a suitably aggressive reaction for a male. This type of response, paired with the feminine traits that I will develop, supports the gender-blurring I contend Morrison works consciously to evoke in this novel.

12. In this way Sethe calls to mind the heroine of another contemporary neo-slave narrative, *Dessa Rose*. In the previous chapter I argued that Dessa derives much of her "power" from the fact that she is a mother.

13. It might be argued that Sethe demonstrates a tendency towards masculine behavior earlier in her decision to kill her child rather than see her remanded to slavery. However, the act might also be viewed as an emotional, "feeling" response to a crisis situation, a response that is not rational or linear.

14. See Sitter's article for an extensive analysis of this scene.

15. The theme of women's community is important in African American literature. Paule Marshall acknowledges it as the source of her inspiration in "The Making of a Writer: From the Poets in the Kitchen," in *Reena and Other Stories* (New York: The Feminist Press, 1983) and contemporary women writers such as Toni Cade Bambara (*The Salt Eaters* [New York: Vintage, 1980]), Gloria Naylor (*The Women of Brewster Place* [New York: Penguin, 1982], and *Mama Day* [New York: Vintage Contemporaries, 1988]) and Ntozake Shange (*for colored girls who have considered suicide/when the rainbow is enuf* [New York: MacMillian Pub-

lishing, 1977]) center their works around the positive ramifications of women nurturing women. For much of this novel, however, Morrison effects a reversal; only Sethe's immediate family members—her mother-in-law and her daughter—serve as community, a community Morrison demonstrates is, ultimately, not sufficiently sustaining.

16. Adrienne Rich, in her chapter "Violence: The Heart of Maternal Darkness," provides a thoughtful discussion of mothers who experience (and sometimes act out) violent emotions towards their children (*Of Woman Born: Motherhood as Experience and Institution* [New York: Norton, 1976]).

17. Anne Goldman takes as her subject the significance of "marking" an enslaved woman's body in " 'I Made the Ink': (Literary) Production and Reproduction in *Dessa Rose* and *Beloved*" (*Feminist Studies* 16 [1990]: 313–30).

18. In an interview with Bessie Jones and Audrey Vinson, Morrison herself notes Sula's masculine traits: "Sula . . . did what men do which is what made her so terrible. I mean she behaves so terribly. (Laughter) It was so terrible because it was askew" (148).

19. In her article entitled "A Ghost of An/Other Chance: The Spinster-Mother in Toni Morrison's *Beloved*," in *Old Maids to Radical Spinsters: Unmarried Women in the Twentieth-Century Novel*, ed. Laura Doan (Chicago: University of Illinois Press, 1991), McKinstry provides a nice reading of possessiveness in the novel, a theme with rich implications relating both to slavery and to motherhood.

20. Others may argue that Beloved herself is the ancestral presence in the novel, particularly as she evokes the Middle Passage and the "sixty million and more" of Morrison's epigraph. However, her character does not fit Morrison's own definition: by the end of the narrative she is neither "benevolent, instructive, [nor] protective" but rather selfish and destructive.

21. This recognition leads Paul D finally to accept himself as a man by his own standards, rather than as a man constantly being measured by society's standards.

22. Interview with Charlie Rose, public television, Spring 1993.

23. Although we must remember Beloved and all that she stands for at the novel's conclusion. Mae Henderson provides an alternate and equally compelling reading of the final passage of the work, suggesting that the last phrase, "This is not a story to be passed on," urges that we not "pass" on the story but rather continue to retell it so that its meaning will not be forgotten. In this reading, the last word "Beloved" surely would refer to the slain child and may have less to do with the thematic significance Morrison ascribes to love.

4

Myth-Making, Myth-Breaking: "Such a thing . . . to marvel over" in J. California Cooper's *Family*

Mothers are something ain't they? They mostly the one person you can count on! All your life . . . if they live. Most mothers be your friend and love you no matter what you do! I bet mine was that way. You ain't never known nobody didn't have one, so they must be something!

> —"Swimming to the Top of the Rain"
> *Homemade Love*, J. California Cooper, 1986

In the previous two chapters I have analyzed works that take as their subject the lives of nineteenth-century American enslaved women. In the chapter on *Dessa Rose* I argue that Sherley Anne Williams empowers her protagonist through a series of reversals; in the chapter on *Beloved* I make a case for gender-blurring, a method of characterization that I posit serves to dramatize the full humanity of enslaved people. Both of these novels are in the vanguard of contemporary American literature because they narrate previously untold, even neglected, stories and contribute to recent efforts to revise and reposition the historical record to ensure greater accuracy. In the company of these novels is a third. J. California Cooper's *Family* shares a number of themes and concerns with Williams' *Dessa Rose* and Morrison's *Beloved*, although it has received considerable less scholarly attention. It is my contention, however, that *Family* parallels these novels and some of the male-authored neo-slave narratives such as *Flight to Canada* and *Middle Passage* in its representation of the joys and perils of slave existence and in its distinctly contemporary message.

When *Family* was published in 1991, it was well received by a number of nonacademic critics, many of whom seemed familiar with Cooper's previous work in drama and short fiction.[1] In a *New York Times Book Review* article, "Everybody's Mother's Ghost," Roy Hoffman praises the novel for its complexity and its energy, stating, "the scene it suggests most strongly is that of a simple stage with a rough-hewn chair at the center, and a lone woman sitting and talking . . . [a]nd the lone woman talking to us, recounting the lives of both the oppressors and the oppressed, is as resilient at the end of her story as she was when it began" (12). Kimberly G. Allen, reviewing for *Library Journal*, commends Cooper's "unorthodox perspective" in *Family* and deems the stories of her protagonist "wrenching" (160). Perhaps the greatest praise for the novel, however, appeared in *Publishers Weekly*. Calling the novel "beautifully textured," the reviewer concludes: "With power and grace, Cooper weaves the dialect, style and myths of the South into a portrait of the hell that was slavery" (Family 64).

The lack of sustained scholarly attention paid to the work, however, is disturbing. The same scholars who write about Alice Walker, Sherley Anne Williams, and Toni Morrison are either unaware of Cooper and her work, are disinterested in her projects, or have relegated her to a second, even third tier of African American women writers. However, Cooper belongs squarely in the midst of revisionist fiction writers and, as the author of one of the most recent neo-slave narratives, deserves special attention for her contribution to the developing genre. J. California Cooper is not an emerging voice in African American literature; she is a fully emerged voice. *Family* powerfully articulates the horrors of slavery while simultaneously celebrating the integrity of black family life from a feminine perspective.

My examination of *Family* begins with the assumption that the myths patriarchal societies invent and embrace are predominantly male.[2] In *Family*, Cooper is creating a new myth, a female myth, to transcend the cosmos of slavery in which she places her characters. Gender distinction is subtly suggested in the opening lines of the novel: "HISTORY. LIVED, NOT WRITTEN, is such a thing not to understand always, but to marvel over" (1). American history as we know it is a decidedly male construct, authored by men in patriarchal language, perpetuated from generation to generation to ensure the survival of the patriarchy. The narrative voice Cooper creates (which is anonymous and genderless at this point) immediately repositions our Western emphasis on *written* history, advocating instead history that is lived, experienced rather than codified. Furthermore, by deemphasizing understanding and substituting wonder (the imperative to "marvel"), the speaker advocates a feminine stance from which to view the world.[3]

Even prior to the opening sentence of the novel Cooper indicates her intention to rewrite history (myth?) by including a vignette about two characters who appear to be outside of time and space. The "epinarrative" of the Earth Mother and the Earth Child serves as a microcosm for the narrative that follows, and is worth quoting in its entirety in order to understand the continuity of theme and imagery that Cooper is able to achieve in the larger narrative.

AND THE EARTH MOTHER ASKED THE EARTH CHILD AS SHE HANDED IT THE SUCCULENT EARTH FRUIT, "AND WHEN DOES A TREE BEAR FRUIT THAT IS NOT ITS OWN?"
AND THE EARTH CHILD THREW BACK ITS BEAUTIFUL HEAD, LAUGHING, SAYING, "NEVER, NEVER . . ." THEN TOOK A HUGE BITE FROM THE HEAVY FULL FRUIT WHICH SENT THE RICH JUICE RUNNING DOWN ITS CHIN, FALLING, FALLING OVER THE MOUNTAINS OF THE EARTH CHILD. ROLLING, ROLLING DOWN AND INTO THE RIVER OF LOVE AND HATE CALLED TEARS. RUNNING, RUNNING EVEN OVER THE FIELDS OF TIME, UNTIL ALL THE JUICES FLOWED TOGETHER AGAIN, BLENDING, INTO THE OCEAN OF HUMAN LIFE.
THE SUN LOOKED DOWN . . . THE MOON PEERED UP. LISTENING, MOVING ON, SAYING, "EVERYONE KNOWS THAT. THAT'S WHAT MAKES A FAMILY!"

This passage retells the paradigmatic story of the fall of humankind. Cooper revises the story of the fall, however, by recasting it as a drama that occurs between a mother and her child and by reconstituting the event as a truly *happy* fall, one that initiates the creation of a new mythic space. Cooper ultimately fills that space with her story of Clora, Always, and their generations of offspring who eventually comprise the whole human family. Moreover, this passage is archetypal in its suggestion of a mother's nurturing of her child, both physically (handing the child the nutritious fruit) and intellectually (actively questioning the child). A second reading of the passage, after the completion of the narrative itself, complexifies the vignette, in that superadded to the mother's question is the burden of her enslaved condition. The Earth Mother's query, then, takes on added poignancy, because a woman who bore children in slavery was like a tree which bore fruit that could not be claimed as its own. Taken in this light, the Earth Child's response seems naive and all-forgiving, but the natural processes she sets into motion by biting into the fruit and spilling its rich juices, and the acquiescence of the sun and the moon, suggest that family and not slavery will be considered the overriding concern of the narrative. The passage is, finally, celebratory, as the possibilities inherent in living as a member of a family parallel the natural fecundity and goodness of the earth.

Although slavery is not Cooper's primary subject matter in *Family*, she pays homage to the slave narrative tradition; the novel reflects many of the conventions of the nineteenth-century American slave narrative.[4] The character who perhaps best illustrates Cooper's debt to the slave narrative tradition is one of the few black males in the text, Sun, Clora's only living male child. Cooper characterizes Sun in a manner that consciously signifies on the life of Frederick Douglass. If, as James Olney asserts, the paradigmatic structure of the slave narrative is the movement from literacy to identity to freedom,[5] and if Douglass' *Narrative of the Life of Frederick Douglass, An American Slave* is the "greatest" American slave narrative "which paradoxically transcends the slave narrative mode while being at the same time its fullest, most exact representative" (Olney 153–54), then Sun's story, incorporated within the larger narrative structure of *Family*, is a virtual retelling of Frederick Douglass' life and experiences. Like Douglass after Mrs. Auld ceases instructing him, Sun "steals" literacy by taking advantage of the friendship his white half-sister Loretta offers. And, as is the case for Douglass, that literacy becomes the key to freedom, enabling Sun to function in society once he has escaped the plantation. Perhaps Sun is most reminiscent of the young Frederick Douglass, however, in his creation of himself, his development into a self-made man once he reaches the North. Working for the white man who owns the waterfront sandwich shack,[6] Sun learns to make himself indispensable and, in his own way, becomes an American entrepreneur, running the shop, helping the owner to open new locations, and eventually marrying into the family. Like Douglass, Sun boosts himself from his oppressed condition, surviving by his wits and his hard work, but as he grows increasingly successful he loses touch with the members of his family who remain enslaved. "Sun had his future pretty good. Because he worked hard. But he also went to worryin less and less bout Always comin to him. She was very light, but not white . . . enough" (125).

Critics have noticed the gap in Douglass' texts (particularly in the first *Narrative*) when it comes to the subject of family and interpersonal relations. Cooper explores that slight through the character of Sun, dramatizing the contrast by choosing to down-play Sun's "American Dream" success story of passing and instead foregrounding Always' story, the story of a woman *and* her family in slavery. It is a story that finally resonates with the American Dream at least as fully as Sun's life and story do.

In addition to acknowledging familiarity with slave narrative conventions, it is apparent that Cooper recognizes the innovations contemporary black women writers have made. It is my intention in the remaining sections of this chapter to suggest that in *Family* J. California Cooper's project is not quite the same as Williams' and Morrison's—the reclamation of the black woman's enslaved past and oppressed humanity. Instead, Cooper is concerned with the creation of a new myth to explore and explain that heritage. She achieves this in three distinct ways: through the narrative voice she creates, through the manner in which she draws attention to the structuring and the passing of time in the narrative, and through her characterization of Always. In each of these areas gender plays a crucial role in the shaping of a new, and decidedly female, mythology of slavery.

According to Holman's *Handbook to Literature*, a myth is defined as "an anonymous story that presents supernatural episodes as a means of interpreting natural events. Myth makes con-

crete and particular a special perception of human beings or a cosmic view" (306). Myths differ from legends and fables in their lack
of emphasis on historical background and didacticism and in their
tendency to foreground the supernatural. Produced by virtually all
culturally connected racial groups, all myths nevertheless share
similar themes: an attempt to explain creation, divinity, religion,
existence, death, and natural phenomena. The *Handbook* points
out that creators of myths endeavor to "arrange their works in
archetypal patterns and present us with narratives that stir us as
'something at once familiar and strange.' They thus give concrete
expression to something deep and primitive in us all" (306). In
other words, myths provide a new way of looking at something
that is already a part of us—an apt description of what Cooper
achieves in *Family*. This novel repositions our twentieth-century
awareness of slavery by focusing not on the "peculiar institution,"
as Frederick Douglass once described slavery, and not on the individual man or woman afflicted by slavery, and not on the historical South as the environs of slavery. Rather, Cooper names her
subject matter in the title of her novel—*Family*—and allows her
narrative to expand that definition to its fullest meaning.

The mythic dimensions of what I have termed "the epinarrative"
cannot be overlooked but serve to prepare the reader for the approach Cooper adopts to tell her main tale. Indeed, the actual narrative begins with an emphasis on mythic or fairy-tale time by
asserting that "you can say 'once upon a time' thousands of times
in one life" (1) and then narrating what is easily recognizable as a
"once upon a time" story—the tale of the Egyptian-Greek man
and the African-Italian man.

In this second short vignette, Cooper sets the stage for her re-
mythologizing by establishing a genealogy for her female protagonists. Shortly into the tale of the Egyptian-Greek man and the
African-Italian man, the story is personalized; the narrator of the
story indicates that the story is autobiographical. Cooper initially
ascribes no gender to the narrative voice she creates; "near my
time, a girl-child was born who was to be my grandmother" (2),
the speaker says in the first reference to personal history. From this
self-referential point, however, the speaker quickly establishes a
female family tree, tracing from the birth of the grandmother the
subsequent birth of the mother. "There was only one person in my

family I knew at that time. My mother. We knew we blonged together cause she had birthed me" (3). The intimacy shared between mother and child is obvious in this passage; the child's perception of the mother's exhaustion is keen, as is the awareness of the pain the mother suffers when the Master of the Land comes into their bed at night.

The relationship this mother and this child shared, as reported from the child's perspective, seems to go beyond the conventional parameters of parent-offspring interaction. Adrienne Rich, in *Of Woman Born: Motherhood as Experience and Institution*, discusses the unusually close bond that exists between a mother and her daughter, concluding that the relationship the two share is characterized by "a knowledge that is subliminal, subversive, preverbal: the knowledge flowing between two alike bodies, one of which has spent nine months inside the other" (220). The insight that Cooper's "voice" provides about the mother's experiences is the reader's first clue that the narrator is female.

Perhaps even more telling with regard to gender than the speaker's remembered relationship with her mother is a statement she makes later in Chapter 1. Reflecting on the forced relationship her mother had with both the Master of the Land and his son, the narrator says, "At twelve years old, I was beginnin to understand life, feeling it" (9). As the opening sentence of the narrative has already established, the emphasis in this text is on feeling, a quality most commonly ascribed to women. This first chapter is marked by an unusually reflective quality; the reader recognizes that the narrator speaks from a distant vantage point of recollection and memory, a position unique in the way it draws attention to how the narrator orders and appropriately emphasizes her story.

Near the end of Chapter 1 we learn that this enigmatic narrative voice has a name—Clora. Significantly, we learn this as Clora learns from her mother how old she is.

She leaned over and drew some lines on the ground. Justa sniffling all the time. I know now there was twelve lines. She say, "That's how old you are, Clora." Her name was Fammy, my name was Clora. I sniffed and said, "Yes mama, mam."

She say, "They gonna count you a woman soon, for sure." I almost smiled cause I thought that might be good but she only cried more, with no sound now. (10)

As exhausted and pained as Clora's mother is, she nevertheless manages to fulfill her role as tradition-bearer for her daughter, ensuring that she know at least a bit of her personal history and simultaneously preparing her for and attempting to shield her from her plight as an enslaved woman of child-bearing age. In some small way, Fammy acts out in this vignette a moment that is at once universal and intensely personal; it may be viewed as a loving gesture, but the gesture remains deeply ambiguous. "Somehow this little piece of time we was havin together was worth anything to me. It was OUR TIME and hadn't nobody appointed it to us" (11), Clora reflects. That time alone together affords Fammy the opportunity to tell Clora that she loves her, but it is also her last chance to be with her daughter; soon after their conversation in the chicken house, as Clora falls asleep, profoundly sad simply because she recognizes her mother's profound sadness, Fammy kills their master and then herself. The gift of an enslaved mother's love that was given so freely in the chicken house was a farewell gift from the woman who could not live any longer as a slave. It also becomes, for Clora, a haunting legacy.

Alone in the dark Clora muses, "Sometime, when life be hittin you with a sledgehammer, it don't stop til it done drove you all the way down, far as you can go . . . to the bottom" (12). Being "done drove . . . all the way down" is precisely the starting point of a myth, because myth can fill the ensuing void and provide, for those who seek it, the will to survive. The lives of Fammy and Clora effectively come to a close the night Fammy kills the master and then herself. Fammy is dead, and the burden of her enslavement is quickly passed on to Clora, who no longer has her tradition-bearer to look to for guidance. "Yes . . . I was a woman at twelve, and sure was one at thirteen years old when I had my first baby for the Master of the Land . . . I *was* my mama, now" (16–17).

Clora relives her mother's legacy in a tragic way, bearing several children for the Master, losing two children to the rigors of enslaved life, and finally reaching a personal breaking point as the burden of being an enslaved mother becomes too heavy to bear alone. Having defied the Mistress by threatening her with a raised poker, Clora recognizes that she will be punished, most likely beaten severely in front of her children, and retreats into nature for solace.

I looked out over them beautiful fields, up into that beautiful sky so full of soft white clouds and the sun so warm and good to shine down on this earth. I saw them tall beautiful trees, weavin and wavin in the winds that come from all crost the earth. I saw birds. Birds what was free to fly off or stay, whatever they wanted . . . free. Better off than me and my slave sisters and brothers. Even the snakes and bugs at my feet was free. That little mosquito was free. But not me. (33–34)

The observations that Clora makes here are a common motif in African American literature focusing on slavery; she looks around, absorbing the beauty of nature, and instead of deriving comfort feels all the more profoundly her own lack of freedom.

Clora makes the same decision as Sethe, the protagonist of Toni Morrison's *Beloved*, determining that her children would be better off dead than lifelong slaves; she further decides that, like her mother, she will kill herself. Clora cannot foresee the consequences of her action, however. Instead of killing the whole family, she succeeds only in poisoning herself. "Do you know what happened?! I died. But my children who I was trying to save . . . lived. Some kind of way they only got sick. Oh very sick, but not dead! I died and left them children and Always in that terrible world, in these bitter times, all alone" (35).

The notion of sacrifice is at stake here, and Cooper seems to question whether an enslaved mother is ever allowed to sacrifice or whether slavery's system of denial extends even this far. Fammy's suicide is less a sacrifice than an act of desperation, but Clora's attempt to take her own life as well as her children's lives may be characterized as a sacrifice gone awry, a sacrifice that ultimately perpetuates the grief that slavery has caused Clora. When she is unsuccessful in taking her children with her beyond the reach of slavery, her plight as an enslaved mother—deeply attached biologically and emotionally to her children yet unable to protect them—is magnified. Clora's plaintive cry, "I was just left" (36) echoes the many cries of enslaved mothers parted from their children by the auction block. Her condition symbolizes the spiritual and psychological condition of all mothers separated from their children by slavery.

But Clora's death is the force that moves the narrative forward; her presence continues to narrate the story. When the transformation from human to narrative voice takes place, Clora assumes a mythic dimension and is allowed, by some divine power,[7] to remain observant of her children. She can foresee the future as it pertains to her "blood" as well. "I knew why I was bein left out. . . . I blive I was left out here so I could watch over my children, my blood, my Always . . . I have seen many, many things. Saw Times change, saw Times stay the same. I understood, at last, many things with a new kind of sense" (36). In death, Clora is afforded a luxury that was denied her in life; she is closer to her children than ever, even though she remains unable to protect them from the evils of slavery. She also seems to possess a sense of calm and a tone of inevitability; she is all-knowing but not omnipotent, neither ghost nor godlike. Cooper is particularly careful to distinguish Clora from a ghost. Clora herself says, "First I must tell you something tho. This dead-but-not-gone thing was not like being a ghost, I don't think. I seem to know all kinds of different knowledge floatin round in space. I couldn't touch nothin, but I could think . . . and I could move" (37).

Clora's close association with nature, her new status as an all-knowing mother, and the sense of timelessness she brings to her narration contribute to the reader's recognition of her mythic quality. Firstly, after her death and as the narrative voice, Clora is at one with nature, sleeping by the side of an ocean and shaping the narrative from her unique vantage point. "The sky is round as the earth! Only bigger, larger, huge, ever so huge that it holds many planets and things. That's why it is endless. It's round" (38). The tone of wonder here is decidedly feminine; already aware that Clora was female, the reader receives several clues from Cooper to ensure that we recognize that the narrative voice retains Clora's gender. The close association with nature is one such clue; also, the emphasis on the roundness of the sky and the earth suggests femininity. Clora has become the Earth Mother (or one of her company) to whom we were introduced in the opening vignette. Thus Clora has transcended ordinary motherhood and has become a sort of Overmother.

Clora has left four children behind: Always, her eldest daughter, Sun, her only son, and Peach and Plum, her two youngest children. Their names suggest the affinity with nature Clora may have had even before her death, and further support a reading that correlates Clora and the Earth Mother of the epinarrative, who is concerned with a fruit-bearing tree.[8] The voice assumes and maintains a sort of maternal authority throughout the narrative; in spite of Clora's extreme position as an enslaved mother separated from her children, in many places her voice cannot be differentiated from the voice of universal motherhood. One such moment occurs near the end of the text, when all of Clora's children except for Plum, who was crushed by Doak Butler's wagon years before, reunite at Always' home after the Civil War. "Chile, I'm tellin you! I was so happy, so glad, so full up with joy! To see my childrens together again. Mine" (218).[9] Clora's joy here is no different from any mother's pride at seeing her children assembled and happy.

The perspective that the narrative voice offers is consonant with that in the epinarrative. A mother's questions, concerns, anxieties, and desire to nurture structure the telling of the tale. Like God who "moves in his own time" (38), Clora also becomes identified with the endless cycle of time and is herself timeless. From her vantage point outside of time she offers a larger-than-life perspective on the earth and its activities, but the narrative voice never loses the preoccupation with slavery and the human family that was initially Clora's legacy from her mother Fammy.

The other primary preoccupation of the narrative voice is time; Cooper's approach to time is easily recognizable as feminine, another clue to the reader that the narrative voice retains Clora's gender after her death. As I have noted, death does not completely efface Clora but places her in a position of remaining observant of her children while restricted, as she was during slavery, from intervening in their lives. She becomes, ironically, an "overseer," responsible not for governing work in the fields but instead, in a more benevolent sense, overseeing the joys and sorrows of her "blood's" day-to-day existence. Death allows Clora, now manifested as the narrative voice, more complete entry into what Julia Kristeva terms "monumental time" (471).[10] Kristeva defines monumental time by associating it specifically with women's cycles and sensibilities.

As for time, female subjectivity would seem to provide a specific measure that essentially retains *repetition* and *eternity* from among the multiple
modalities of time known through the history of civilizations.

  . . . there are cycles, gestation, the eternal recurrence of a biological
rhythm which conforms to that of nature and imposes a temporality
whose stereotyping may shock, but whose regularity and unison with what
is experienced as extrasubjective time, cosmic time, occasion vertigious
visions and unnameable *jouissance*. (472–73)

Kristeva arrives at her definition of monumental time by placing
it against conventional notions of time—time as linear and chron-
ological, what she calls the "time of history" (473).

It has already been abundantly demonstrated that this kind of temporality
is inherent in the logical and ontological values of any given civilization,
that this temporality renders explicit a rupture, an expectation, or an anguish which other temporalities work to conceal. It might also be added
that this linear time is that of language considered as the enunciation of
sentences (noun + verb; topic-comment; beginning-ending), and that this
time rests on its own stumbling block—death. (473)

It is important to note that an enslaved person was completely
victimized by time; as Clora says of her mother, "Didn't have her
own self no time" (6). Unable to "own" herself, Fammy (and all
men and women in her condition) had no control over time—how
she spent it or whether its passing was monumental or linear.
"[T]ime didn't mean anything to my people, exceptin it was hard
times all the time" (3). This is perhaps most clearly dramatized
when Fammy teaches Clora her age by showing her a small pile of
stones, each representing a year of her life. Using stones to mark
the passage of time was one way illiterate slaves were able to account for the passing years.

But although the years passed and the mounds of stones grew,
little changed. In Clora's words, " 'tomorrow . . . tomorrow' was
goin to be just the same thing all over again. A new name for the
same day, over and over again" (7). Cooper's depiction of slave
time may be perceived as both linear and circular (monumental).
It was linear in that, for most enslaved persons, life was a clearly
delineated cycle of birth, hard work, and death. The birth of an
enslaved child was a celebrated event only for the owner, who

looked forward greedily to his increased wealth. Many enslaved mothers, like Harriet Jacobs, prayed for their infants' deaths, hoping to spare them the anguish of enslavement; many enslaved men and women, in fact, looked forward to death, believing that it would finally bring them rest and a well-deserved heavenly reward. For these enslaved persons, time inevitably marched forward in a straight line, marking the steps from the field to the graveyard.

In spite of a situationally imposed emphasis on the linear movement from birth to death, the passage of time must have seemed circular as well to the enslaved Africans. Indeed, this narrative exhibits a hyperawareness of time; frequently the reader is overtly reminded of the swift passage of time. Kristeva's notion of monumental time is grounded in the assumption that time, as perceived by women, mirrors the biological cycle and the rhythms of nature. The problem in using this term to discuss time in a slave narrative is immediately apparent; the biological cycle of a slave woman made her an unwilling accomplice in the perpetuation of her condition and the rhythms of nature were not to be enjoyed by the enslaved persons but merely served to remind them of the duties of the season: "planting-time, harvest-time" in the words of Frederick Douglass in his 1845 *Narrative*. The passing of the seasons helped the enslaved man or woman keep track of his or her age, but was also a poignant reminder for the enslaved person who did not know the actual date of birth and for whom the passage of time merely meant the accumulation of duties. Therefore, awareness of time as cyclical, as indicated in the quotation above, merely serves to suggest entrapment in a cycle beyond the slaves' control. If " 'tomorrow . . . tomorrow' [is] the just the same thing all over again," then individuals like Fammy and Clora are caught in a vortex that perpetuates their misery.

If time for the enslaved person had both a linear inevitability and a smothering circularity, then the creation of a new mythology of slavery opens the space for a radical reconception of time. By removing Clora from the world of slavery by death but by preventing her from entering the afterlife, Cooper positions her narrator as the keeper of a new time, time that Cooper posits as an alternative to linear or monumental time. Whereas the slaves' conventional perspective of time may be described as centripetal, drawing them more and more deeply towards the center, a core of

hard work, servitude and heartache lessened only by the promise
of death, Cooper's "new" mythology of time seems to flow cen-
trifugally, moving away from the center that is slavery and across
time freely and fluidly. As Clora's children grow older and spread
apart geographically, Clora is able to move effortlessly to be with
them in spirit. "I didn't know much about my kind of time early
on, when I would think on one or other of my children, swift as
a second I find I am where I can see the one I'm thinking bout"
(119). The narrative, from Clora's death and the beginning of her
reporting, is sprinkled with phrases such as "In the meantime,"
phrases that mark the telling of her tale. Frequently, as at the end
of Chapter 4, she tells the reader that she is "ahead of [her] story
again" (63), emphasizing both the distance from which Clora observes and the obvious relish she takes in relating the story of Always and the other family she has left behind. "My space, where
I was, was warm and proud of my child-woman. See? I knew freedom was near, I could see it from here" (118).

The privileged perspective Cooper affords her narrator is her
most innovative stylistic achievement. By positioning the narrator
of this story of slavery first as an actual character in the drama
and then removing her from the narrative, Cooper is successful in
making the reader experience for a brief moment the wrench a
slave mother felt when her child was sold from her. The reader
absorbs the grief Clora articulates at being separated from her children and the powerlessness she feels at being unable to protect
them from the evils of slavery. Cooper establishes an intimacy between the reader and the narrator by allowing the narrator to address the reader while relating the narrative and by pointing up
instances where the narrator consciously refers to the telling of the
tale. Most remarkable, however, is her deliberate choice to gender
the narrative voice. The reader is seldom able to forget that the
narrator is the mother of the characters she observes and chroni-
cles, a fact that renders the story all the more powerful because it
is not merely the story of an enslaved mother; it is also the enslaved
mother's story. Clearly drawing on her experiences as a woman
and a mother during slavery, Clora informs the project with a distinctly feminine energy. She has absolute authority over her story,
something denied to her in slavery. That authority, coupled with
her release from the confines of both linear and monumental time,

empowers her to be the agent responsible for creating a new mythology, a mythology that changes our twentieth-century perception of slavery by focusing on the individual and her family relations rather than on the institution itself. The narrative voice Cooper creates becomes the new voice in the telling of the enslaved person's story, a voice that is at once personal and universal. Instead of universally white and male, however, that voice is undeniably black and maternal.

It is important to note that Clora is not part of the new mythology that we see in *Family*. Rather, she is the myth-shaper, our access to the myth—a griot of sorts. At the center of the new myth is Always, the enslaved girl who inherits her mother's life. In Always, Cooper creates a new type of African American mythic figure, one who is not enslaved by the land but is almost indistinguishable from it. By the end of the narrative she is larger than life, more myth than person, able to rejuvenate barren land, inspire hopeless lives,[11] and endure with dignity to see the day when she is legally emancipated.

At first it looks as if Always will be caught up in the same cycle of abuse and suicide by which her mother and her mother's mother were victimized. But Always possesses an intuition and a will that her maternal forebears lacked. She experiences a turning point early in her life that changes her perspective on slavery and triggers a whole set of survival skills she was previously unaware of possessing.

> Always didn't know she was pretty. It's somethin you may not know, but most slaves that ain't in the house in a regular job, never see a mirror. Never get to see what they look like. Ain't that somethin? Can live all your life and never know what your own face looks like! . . . But, bein in that big house so much she [Always] got to see herself and it came to her that she was white. Most white as her mistress. Always got mad and stayed mad from then on. (41)

Always' recognition, first that she is pretty and secondly that her skin is almost as fair as the mistress', provides her with a sense of self-awareness that she uses to validate herself as a person.[12] This newfound awareness distracts her from the realities of her day-to-day life as an enslaved person long enough for her emotions to quicken and she "g[ets] mad and stay[s] mad" (41). While Always' anger could serve to associate her with her grandmother Fammy, who killed her master with a pitchfork, the reader would do well to remember that Fammy's behavior is characterized more as help-lessness and desperation than as anger. Before the deed she tells Clora, "Mama can't even help herself" (10), and her actual attack on the master is described in very matter-of-fact terms. Always, on the other hand, brims with emotion; Cooper depicts Always as very well balanced, negotiating carefully between head and heart. The ability to do this affords her stamina that both Fammy and Clora lacked and allows her to endure the double jeopardy of being a woman and being enslaved. She is also a mother—both her genuine spirit of feeling and her close association with nature and the land identify her as an Earth-Mother figure and she functions as an "othermother"[13] to her younger siblings, although to them she seems "mean and serious all the time" (49), the result of the re-sponsibilities with which she is burdened.

The land itself assumes a mythic quality in Cooper's narrative, and the author is careful to implicate the "Masters of the land"— white men—in her myth-breaking. Like the enslaved Africans who work it, the land and its resources have been exploited to the point of exhaustion. Cooper emphasizes the destruction by deliberately associating Always with nature, its inherent freedom and its life-giving quality. In fact, Always' reclaiming of the land and its re-sources is one of the key elements in the creation of the new myth. "She put out her arm and her hand sought a leaf, a little flower bud and pressed it to her nose. The smell was free" (78). When she is unable to spare the birds a few morsels from her own meagre food supply, Always scatters petals, saying, " 'I don't have no food to give you today, but I'll give you some love, little bird,' and dropped the young petals down to the free bird" (80). Even as a child Always envies the freedom the birds have and attempts to coopt some of their free-spiritedness by spending a moment in their company before departing with Doak Butler.

The only time we witness Always falter occurs when she is sold to Doak Butler. Parted from her family and not even allowed to kiss her beloved sister Plum good-bye, Always is fully initiated into the evil of slavery at the time of her sale. The moment she realizes that Plum, who has hidden under the wagon to be with her, has

been crushed by the wheel base and has slowly bled to death, is
the most painful in the text and is surely the most painful in Always' life. The fact that Doak Butler is raping Always at the same
time that Plum is suffering soundlessly nearby merely intensifies
the horror that drives Always into the stance of isolation and indifference she assumes when she reaches her new home.

Always had, from her first walkin and seein times, loved trees and flowers,
sunshine and birds and things. Now, lookin at the yard and shabby fence
of her new home, she felt nothin but a weary emptiness. The trees looked
mean and broodin. The yard was like a empty, dead desert full of death.
There was no comfort in the huge trees full of birds. They looked stiff,
unreal and unfriendly, like the whole place had been lost and was just
standin there to become her grave, not her home. She looked at the land
where it stretched out, tryin to see the end of life. (90)

The imagery Cooper creates clearly suggests that the Butler
homestead is barren; there is an emptiness associated with both
Doak Butler and his land. When they arrive Doak speaks with
pride about what he owns. "He grinned, stretched out his arm,
pointin, wavin at his land. 'This here is all mine! Thirty-five acres!
Good soil! And we gonna fix this house up too!' " (90). He qual-
ifies only by saying, "Right now it don't show up so good" (90).
But Always, even through her pain and suffering, registers the fact
that the land is neither productive nor promising, at least under
Doak's authority. He is portrayed as the patriarch, surveying all
that he owns and envisioning colonization, saying, "But with a
wife, and you, a sturdy slave with a lotta good years and strong
suckers in you, we gonna one day stretch out to far as you can
see!" (90) Although he appears to speak inclusively, including his
wife and his slave, ironically, he is addressing Always, another
piece of his property.
Interestingly, the land belonging to Always' previous master was
not productive either. "Things wasn't goin too well on that farm.
Land dryin up, wearin out" (56). When the patriarch of this property (ironically referred to as Master of the Land) is killed by
Clora's mother, his son inherits his property and his lecherous lifestyle. The reader is told that he "picked up a dis-ease on one of
them trips to somewhere tryin to sell some of the slaves. He passed

it round to some of his own women slaves at home" (57). The dissolute quality of life is obvious, and it is no accident that Always remains free from disease although the new master uses her sexually as his father had done with her mother. Instead of seeing her become debased through her association with the slaveholding whites, we witness Always becoming more closely allied with the land itself. She avoids the disease, and she is even able to manipulate her horrific introduction to Doak Butler's homestead into something that encourages her to live and to thrive. In fact, it may be argued that being sold to Doak Butler provides Always with the opportunity to forge a meaningful sense of personhood for herself.

White men are clearly implicated in the destruction and decay of the land and its natural resources. Doak Butler specifically is to blame for the crushed spirit Always brings to his homestead, but he is also responsible for providing her with the impetus to fight back. The land becomes both her tool and her weapon. Thinking about where to bury Plum, Always abhors the thought of placing her in the soil of Doak Butler's wasted farmland. But she becomes a colonizer in her own right when she thinks of a plan that will subvert some of Doak's authority. "A place, a secret place, she would find to bury her little sister, the end of her family. And that secret piece of land she would make hers. She'd steal it!" (91) Bidding good-bye to her sister, the "end of her family," Always sets out to forge a new sort of family for herself, a kinship with the land that she has always cherished. Although she initially professes to hate Doak Butler and his land, she resolves to live, a promise that rekindles the fire of emotion we have seen previously as characterizing Always. " 'I will live. I will live to destroy them like they's destroyed me and my mama and my family.' She looked at the land again. 'I'm gonna destroy you too' " (91).

Initially Always' plan involves merely "stealing" a small plot of land as a resting place for her sister. As her tenure as Doak's slave continues, however, Always begins the practice of naming pieces of land for children she is forced to bear for Doak, children he eventually sells away. "So there was fields named Lester, Ruby, and Lark, and a whole lotta cows named Satti" (135). In this small way Always is able to delegitimize Doak Butler's absolutist claims to the property that he owns and stake a small claim of her own. Indeed, the refrain, "She just looked over the land, always" (98), may be viewed as the shaping motif of the second half of the narrative.

Being in touch with nature and sharing a sort of maternal bond with the land her blood has purchased are qualities through which Cooper insists on Always' femininity. However, the way that Cooper genders her protagonist is not that simple. Always resembles Sethe, Morrison's heroine in *Beloved*, whose character is developed by means of gender-blurring. The way that Always aggressively works the land, forcing it to become more fertile and more prosperous, characterizes her as a gentleman farmer.

[S]he went to find a hoe and went out to the land to work it, to see and feel it. The sun was hot upon her back, the sweat began to drip from the sides of her face to her breast as she hoed in good rhythm, easily, smoothly, turnin the dark, rich earth over. She stopped now and again, bent to feel and turn the soil in her hands, feeling it was good soil. Ever once and awhile she would look thoughtfully over the land . . . [j]ust thinkin of what the land could bear. (99)

In the new myth, Cooper creates an African American heroine who is not enslaved by the land but who becomes one with it. Always' "look[ing] over the land" evolves into working the land— the duty of a common field slave—which, in turn, leads to her feeling the land. Eventually, Doak Butler's barren land is transformed into a self-sustaining estate, with Always at the helm. Her efforts puzzle Poon, who fails to understand that Always' attempt to make the land productive mirrors her efforts at making meaning in her own life. Ultimately, the land that Always names for her sold babies becomes her life and she refuses to be parted from it; although she is lonely, she even spurns relationships with men. "[H]er heart made no choice. She would not leave the land she felt was hers" (149).

In addition to resuscitating Doak Butler's farm, Always manages to provide for herself. She tells Poon early in her stay at Doak's that she wants her own garden to tend, not an unusual request for a slave, as many supplemented the meagre livelihood provided to them by the master with the fruits of their own labor. But Cooper draws attention to the significance Always places on her own garden. Always says, "I'll eat what food everybody else grows and eats. I want silver money to come out from my garden. I wants silver and gold money from what I grow" (110). The statement clarifies Always' entrepreneurial plans and ties her to Sun, who works in the North for material security; however, in its evocation of money literally growing on trees, is also mythic, suggesting a new order of prosperity and independence for the enslaved black female.

Indeed, Always' work with and on the land affords her a degree of freedom many enslaved persons lacked. She journeys to neighboring farms to consult other workers and farmers, buying seeds and comparing methods and recipes. And when Sue, Doak's young wife, becomes pregnant, Always combines questions about pregnancy and childbirth with her inquiries about farming, demonstrating that her foremost concern is life, both the life of the land and human life.

In addition to portraying Always as an independent farmer, working the land and increasing its productivity, Cooper also suggests that there is something of the trickster about Always. As in some African myths, in Cooper's new mythology the trickster is a woman and a mother. When Always gives birth to her first child by Doak, a son she names Soon, she does so unassisted, a detail in keeping with the independent spirit she has worked so hard to cultivate. This detail, however, also allows her to swap her fair-skinned child for the baby Doak's wife has delivered twenty-four hours earlier.[14] The boys grow up side by side, best friends as children but increasingly distant as they become aware of the difference in their stations in life. The children are well into adulthood before Always reveals her deed. Here the trickster is characterized not by greed or deception but by love; as Always demonstrates over the course of the years, she is generous enough to love both boys as her own, although it pains her that she is never able to acknowledge her biological son, the son who is reaping the advantages of being white in a white man's world.

It would be an oversight, however, to fail to acknowledge an element of self-preservation present in Always' reunion with her biological son. After showing Doak, Jr., where some of his father's money is buried, Always thinks, "Gave birth to you here. Now you gon take the gold and give me a home for my life" (192). When she reveals their true relationship, pointing out the "mole" they share as proof of their biological connection, she is able to extort what she wants from her son. All she asks for is ownership of a plot of land and the means to provide a small home for herself. She does not want to leave the Butler homestead but wishes to live there independently. "I know this dirt like my own blood runnin in my body. . . . This land is part of my body. My roots is deep in this ground" (202). In a reversal similar to those which I have argued characterize Dessa Rose's relationships with whites, Always exerts power over her own son, a man who is, both in society's eyes and in his own, white. "He felt like the slave!" (203). But what Doak is slave to is his materialistic desire for his father's wealth. Always, on the other hand, is free, no longer enslaved and also free once she publicly acknowledges both her deed and her child.[15]

The novel ends not with Always, who refuses to leave the land when freedom comes to the South, but with Clora, in her role as the narrative voice. The voice structuring and commenting on Always' story is consistently vigorous throughout the novel, suffering with the children as they endure slavery and its evils and jubilant when they overcome seemingly impossible obstacles. Near the end of the novel, the narrative voice seems to merge with Always, saying of the child Always will have in freedom with Tim, her black husband, "I was excited cause this child we could keep. It was ours!" (211). This moment marks the fulfillment of Clora's (and Cooper's) new mythology; the enslaved woman, finally free, will bear a child who will be unequivocally hers, thus achieving the total affirmation of self—body and spirit—that Clora and the generations of enslaved women before her were denied. From this point the narrative voice begins to weaken, and it is thoroughly diminished by the end of the tale. "I tried my best to get on way from here. Tired of livin without livin. But try as I might, I didn't go nowhere . . . I HAD to stay round to see what would happen again, to my blood. My blood. My family" (229).

Clora insists throughout the narrative that what she is witnessing and recording is the process of her family's blood spreading out. "My blood ran like it was let loose from a stream into the river, into the ocean. It ran" (63), says the narrator early in the narrative. Here Cooper seems consciously to allude to Langston Hughes' poem "The Negro Speaks of Rivers." Like Hughes' speaker, Clora

celebrates black association with the land and its myths and dramatizes a story in which enslaved or marginalized characters endure
through the mythic reordering of their experience. But also like
Hughes' speaker, who appears to witness from a distance, Clora
finds herself increasingly distanced from her "blood," which flows
with renewed vigor once slavery is abolished in the United States.
The final pages of the novel dramatize her exhaustion; Clora seems
too weary to keep up with her "blood."

> I was so tired in my soul. Tired of all I had lived and seen, now, I was
> tired from all I had stayed round to see. I saw my blood spread out all
> over into such places I never dreamed of in my wildest dreams. Makes me
> know, if from one woman all these different colors and nationalities could
> come into bein, what must the whole world be full of?! (230)

What Clora ponders as she grows more removed from the myth
she has set in motion is the continuity of life and family she inaugurated when she gave birth to the daughter she named Always.

A significant revision occurs on the final pages of the narrative.
Clora, recognizing that she is growing weaker and more tired with
each passing moment, slumbers and awakens fifteen years later, in
1933. Upon awakening, she is shocked to realize how much she
has missed, not only with regard to her own kin but also in terms
of world events. Suddenly she is forced to call into question her
previous perception of time (that "tomorrow . . . tomorrow" was
always the same day); now she marvels, "Every day is new!" (230).
Clora's realization that every day is indeed a new day demonstrates
her newfound understanding of the fact that all races of people
have suffered, not just the black race. "You all had had wars and
famine, depressions and recessions, union fights, labor horrors,
poverty worse, look like, then some slavery. For all colors this
time!" (229).

This moment of insight comprises the fullest expression of a sentiment that Clora expressed much earlier in the narrative: "People
is human" (53). As the narrator of a myth not fully her own, Clora
betrays some uncertainty at points in the story; she appears to be
able to foresee future events, but she is not confident in her appreciation of what the outcome of those events will be. Finally, she is
confident—confident in her daughter Always, who has made a

truly human life for herself in spite of the inhumanities of slavery, and confident that she will finally be able to thrust aside the ambiguous burden she has carried since her death, the burden of being a dismembered voice chronicling the story of her kin and rest in peace.

Peace is, indeed, the overriding sentiment at the conclusion of the narrative, and is the final component in J. California Cooper's mythopoeia. However, it is violence that undergirds many of our Western myths; we commonly view the world as the battleground for the elements of good and evil, and our literary myths reflect our penchant for war. Virgil boldly proclaims the great theme of the *Aeneid* in his opening line: *Arma virumque cano* ("I sing of arms and of a man"); Homer begins the *Iliad* with the account of the quarrel between Achilles and Agamemnon, two men who battle the Trojans over the beautiful Helen. At the center of *Beowulf* is the epic battle between Beowulf and Grendel, a battle designed to showcase the hero's courage when confronted by overwhelming physical adversity. For whatever reason, violence and war seem far more interesting subject matter than peace, which is, ironically, the anticipated outcome of any battle.

Violence is at the heart of many neo-slave narratives as well. Sethe kills her child and warns the reader at the end of *Beloved* that "This is not a story to pass on," presumably because of its gory premise; Dessa Rose kills white men leading the coffle. These actions propel the stories forward to their resolution.

Cooper's message is different, however. By repositioning our customary association between blood and violence and placing a new emphasis on "blood" as kin, Cooper draws attention to peace both as the subject of and as the legacy of her myth, a fact she underscores by placing an enslaved female who is both an other-mother and a mother at the center of that myth. She also establishes a precedent for storytelling with the narrative voice she creates and suggests the eternal quality of her tale by reiterating the title in the final word of the novel, insisting that this new myth must not only be told but must be retold, Always. The universalizing conclusion Cooper crafts reaches out to readers of all colors as we, like Clora, recognize that this is not a story only about African Americans but is a story of the human race, a story in which each one of us has a stake. "Cause all these people livin are brothers and sisters and cousins. All these beautiful different colors! We! . . . We the human Family. God said so! FAMILY!" (231).

NOTES

1. To date, Cooper is perhaps best known as a writer of short fiction. Her volumes of short stories include *A Piece of Mine* (1984), *Homemade Love* (1986), which received the American Book Award in 1989, *Some Soul to Keep* (1987), and *The Matter Is Life* (1991). Additionally, Cooper was named Black Playwright of the Year in 1978 for her play *Strangers*.

2. Deborah E. McDowell touches on this point in her article "In the First Place: Making Frederick Douglass and the Afro-American Narrative Tradition," in *Critical Essays on Frederick Douglass*, ed. William L. Andrews (Boston: G. K. Hall & Co., 1991). Discussing the story of Adam and Eve as the first Genesis myth, McDowell describes what she terms Adam's "firstness," a fact that of necessity dictates Eve's "secondariness," and notes that "[t]his myth, associated with the male story, with the name and the Law of the Father, represses the name and the word of the mother" (194).

3. For a thorough discussion of the ways gender influences world view, see *Women's Ways of Knowing: The Development of Self, Voice, and Mind*, ed. Mary Field Belenky et al. (New York: Basic Books, 1986). I use this work in Chapter 3 to establish differences in how males and females relate to the world around them and to each other, and some of the material is applicable here.

4. These characteristics include cruel masters who physically and sexually abuse the female slaves on their plantations, ineffectual white women who ignore their husbands' indiscretions with female slaves and who are alternately generous and cruel to the female slaves and their offspring, tragic mulatto children, the separation of slave children from their natural mothers, the presence of an "othermother" figure who cares for slave children in the quarters, attempts—both unsuccessful and successful—to defeat the cruel master/mistress by wit or craft, attempts—both unsuccessful and successful—at flight to freedom, and hardships after the abolition of slavery.

5. See Olney, " 'I Was Born': Slave Narratives, Their Status as Autobiography and as Literature," in *The Slave's Narrative*, ed. Charles T. Davis and Henry Louis Gates, Jr. (New York: Oxford University Press, 1985, 148–75). I discuss Olney's literacy-identity-freedom paradigm in Chapter 1.

6. It is interesting to note that the white man's name is Mr. Du Bois.

Perhaps Cooper is having a bit of fun signifying the great African American hero W.E.B. Du Bois, whose personal philosophy suggests prioritizing the intellect over emotions. Cooper's use of Du Bois' name in this context may serve to evoke the choice that Sun has made in neglecting to communicate with his family once he reaches the North, or she may be evoking the name satirically, given W.E.B. Du Bois' position on segregationalist politics and Sun's "passing."

    7. We know that Cooper has posited a universe that is governed by God, but she provides no explanation for what happens to Clora. Clora herself refers several times to God; she wonders what accounts for her nebulous existence after death, saying, "Now God didn't say nothin to me" (36), and recognizes that she is not God: "I could not see everything. God is the only One Who sees everything" (51). She also dwells on the beauty of nature, attributing it to God's work.

    8. The exception in Clora's scheme of naming her children after the natural world is, of course, Always, the child who becomes the protagonist of the narrative. Of her naming Clora tells us, "I knew no matter what life had in store for either me or my baby I would love her always. So . . . that's what I named her . . . Always" (19). When Always is bought by Doak Butler and brought to his home, Poon—cynical after years of slavery—says upon learning Always' name, "Always. That a kind of foolishness name. But mayhap you was named right . . . cause your life always gonna be just what it is now, here, where you is" (96). Always proves Poon wrong, not only bettering life for herself and her son but for Poon and others as well, thus reversing Poon's fatalistic interpretation of her name and restoring it to her mother's original intent.

    9. The question of how Cooper's narrative voice creates audience is an interesting one, but too complex to explore fully here. However, it is apparent that Cooper wishes her reader to recognize his or her own stake in the mythic reworking she imagines because she allows Clora to address her listener directly as "Chile"—thus implying that the reader/listener is one of her own. This suggestion also reinforces Cooper's overriding thematic issue, family.

    10. The term "monumental time" has come to be commonly associated with Julia Kristeva, the French theorist and psychoanalyst. However she points out in her essay "Women's Time" that the term rightly belongs to Nietzsche.

    11. It is important to note that Always works to better not only her own life but the lives of those around her; her impact is far-reaching. For instance, Poon seems visibly to grow younger after Always' arrival at Doak Butler's, and Jason, strapped onto a horse to assist in cultivating the land, gains physical strength and the will to live.

12. It could be argued, of course, that the significance Always accords to her fair skin is her way (consciously or subconsciously) of repressing her blackness.

13. For an excellent discussion of the role of the "othermother" in the black community, see Patricia Hill Collins' "The Meaning of Motherhood in Black Culture and Black Mother/Daughter Relationships" (*SAGE* 4:2 [1987]: 3–10). In part, Collins argues the "Black women's feelings of responsibility for nurturing the children in their own extended family networks have stimulated a more generalized ethic of care where Black women feel accountable to all the Black community's children" (5). According to Hill, most "othermother" figures are either grandmothers or older women not related to the children by blood; in this respect Always, as the oldest sibling, is a somewhat unusual "othermother" figure. However, to argue that she does not function in this capacity is to overlook the primary role of nurturance she assumes when Clora dies.

14. Always' scheme here is similar to Roxy's in Mark Twain's 1894 novel *Pudd'nhead Wilson*, although the remarkable difference between the two baby-swapping plots is the black woman's triumph of wit and independence in Cooper's novel.

15. Cooper perhaps uses this episode to further comment on the nature of the American Dream and blacks' role in that dream. Doak Jr., ostensibly a white man, is enslaved by his greed, whereas Always is able to secure for herself a comfortable, well-furnished home (easily recognizable as one of the primary goals of the American Dream) by the end of the narrative. The episode also recalls the admonition Frederick Douglass and other nineteenth-century slave narrators gave their readers—that slavery is detrimental for whites as well as for blacks.

5

"So Many Relatives": Twentieth-Century Women Meet Their Pasts

> In women there is always more or less of the mother who makes everything all right, who nourishes, and who stands up against separation; a force that will not be cut off but will knock the wind out of the codes.
>
> —Hélène Cixous

CORREGIDORA: BIRTH OF THE SELF

In a 1982 interview with Charles Rowell, Gayl Jones issued a challenge to all writers interested in American slavery: "[T]he writer [must] say something different or explore some new dimension of the Afro-American slave experience that hasn't already been done and done finely by Ernest Gaines in *The Autobiography of Miss Jane Pittman* and Margaret Walker in *Jubilee.* . . . It's a genre I think and a truth of the American experience; what are the truths about it that haven't already been told?" (42).

As we have seen, a number of black women writers working in the 1980s and 1990s met Jones' ultimatum by producing works that cast slave women in never-before imagined roles. However, Jones was not merely issuing a challenge but was seeking to establish her own work as an example; while not precisely a neo-slave narrative, her 1975 novel *Corregidora* has at its heart an embedded slave narrative.[1] Telling the story of a twentieth-century blues singer who grows to recognize the ramifications of her enslaved heritage, Jones attempts to "say something different" about slavery by depicting the legacy of psychosexual abuse that black women have inherited.

Chronologically, *Corregidora* is the earliest novel considered in this study and is an excellent choice for the way it foregrounds the revisionary efforts of later writers dealing with the African American slave experience. It is my contention that in 1975 Jones was not so much revising gender roles as emphasizing stereotypical sex roles (specifically, the "macho" male and the female not in touch with her own sexuality) to explore how slavery's legacy insidiously infects generations ostensibly removed from its immediate effects. When Ursa Corregidora loses her reproductive capabilities, she also loses the means by which to carry out her ancestors' imperative to "make generations" (41). In other words, she will not mother a child to continue the Corregidora women's tradition of bearing witness to the brutality of slavery. Instead, she must inaugurate her own tradition. She eventually discovers that the creation of her own personal blues song will enable her to give birth to a fully integrated, individuated self.

Many reviewers of the novel praised the way that Jones in *Corregidora* is able to negotiate a fine line between sexuality and spirituality, between uncertainty and the profound need to know, between loss and discovery. In *Newsweek*, Margo Jefferson states that "hatred, love and desire wear the same face" in the novel (85). John Updike, in the *New Yorker*, celebrates Ursa's attempt "to transcend a nightmare black consciousness and waken to her own female, maimed humanity" (82), and John Alfred Avant in *New Republic* says of Jones and her first novel, "[She] avoids ideology, although her novel deals implicitly with racial and feminist issues ... but it is not an indictment of white America, not a woman-in-search-of-identity novel, nor is it a woman-as-sex-object novel" (27).

In declaring the novel as "simply, about the awful complexity of one woman's life," Avant is being awfully simplistic. His appraisal that *Corregidora* is not a "woman-in-search-of-identity" novel or a "woman-as-sex-object" novel completely misses the mark—it is both of these. Precisely because of her lack of identity Ursa finds herself drawn to men in a blind attempt at following the Corregidora women's command to "make generations." Jones dramatizes this point by including in her novel the frank language of sexuality, the language that characterizes Ursa's intimate relationships with Mutt and Tadpole. In fact, the use of graphic, provocative language is Jones' great literary innovation; she not only opens up new territory by taking as her subject both a woman's sexuality and sexual abuse, but she adopts the vernacular of raw sexuality to explore her topic.[2]

Jones' insistent emphasis on Ursa's sexuality directly revises Harriet Jacobs' account of her own life in *Incidents in the Life of a Slave Girl*. Jones replaces the discrete and circumlocutious language Jacobs was forced to adopt in deference to her white audience with sexually charged language, particularly flaunting the verb "fuck" and the noun "pussy," the only word used to refer to Ursa's vagina. Because these terms are often associated with men and their relationship to female sexuality, it might appear initially that Ursa's use of these words suggests power and liberation; even Ursa's maternal grandmother and great-grandmother adopt them as they describe their sexual enslavement at the hands of Corregidora, the Brazilian coffee plantation owner who was their master.[3] However, upon closer examination, the language is not liberating.[4] Instead, particularly in Ursa's case, the words create a mindset of enslavement, as Ursa herself appropriates the language, relating how she is "fucked" first by Mutt and then by Tadpole and also by telling each man that her "pussy" belongs to him.

The end result is that Ursa, because of her foremothers' legacy, sees herself as nothing more than a "pussy" to be "fucked," and thus allows herself to be enslaved both by her ancestors' legacy and by the men with whom she enters into relationships. Nowhere is this more telling than when Mutt threatens to interrupt her singing performance at Happy's Cafe and "sell" her: " 'One a y'all wont to bid for her? Piece a ass for sale' " (159). Here Mutt adopts the rhetoric of the auction block, perhaps even imitating the nineteenth-century white master auctioning one of his slave women.[5] Ursa, numb to the implications of Mutt's actions because of her own conditioned response to herself as a sex object, a "piece a ass," responds only with uncertainty; should she tell Tadpole so that he can protect her and, if she does, will she look ridiculous if Mutt is only bluffing?

Mutt is not the only man whom Ursa allows to victimize her. Even Tadpole, who nurtures her after her tragic accident,[6] sexualizes her and their relationship with little apparent regard for Ursa as a person. As early as their wedding night Tadpole begins to resemble Mutt.

> "I won't have you singing on your wedding day."
> "You won't start that too, will you?" . . .
> "Sing for me here," he said. He unbuckled his pants and lay down on the bed. I sang for him, then we made love. (68)

Consciously or unconsciously, Tadpole gives every indication of having fallen into the same pattern of jealous behavior that ruined the relationship Ursa shared with Mutt. The demand, "Sing for me here," is *his* imperative; it is his definitive statement to Ursa that *his* needs come first, and what he needs of Ursa is sex.

Narratively, Jones works to suggest Ursa's victimization by and, in fact, enslavement to the men she becomes involved with by fusing scenes that take place between Ursa and Tadpole with scenes between Ursa and Mutt. Repeatedly the reader notes abrupt transitions—intimate moments between Ursa and Tadpole blur into memories of her relationship with Mutt. As Tadpole's character deteriorates and the reader observes him becoming more like Mutt, lines spoken by Mutt, which Ursa recalls while with Tadpole, begin to resonate as if Tadpole himself speaks them. Further enriching the theme of psychosexual abuse as it is dramatized in *Corregidora* is the fact that Mutt's language, later echoed by Tadpole, is originally the language of Ursa's grandmother and great-grandmother,[7] thus indicating, as I will later argue, that Ursa's maternal ancestors were in some way complicitous in perpetuating if not their actual enslavement, then the mentality of victimization that enslaves them, and which they pass on both to Ursa and, before her, to her mother.

Indeed, Ursa Corregidora's maternal forebears lie at the core of her identity crisis. Patricia Hill Collins, in her article entitled "The Meaning of Motherhood in Black Culture and Black Mother/ Daughter Relationships," argues that "the experience of motherhood can provide Black women with a base of self-actualization, status in the Black community, and a reason for social activism" (4).[8] Ursa's female relations, however, suggest—insist, in fact— that there is no role other than mother for her. *"The important thing is making generations"* (22); later they tell her, *"We got to burn out what they put in our minds, like you burn out a wound. Except we got to keep what we need to bear witness. That scar that's left to bear witness. We got to keep it as visible as our blood"* (72). Instead of bequeathing to Ursa a foundation for self-knowledge and a drive that comes from *within* for social justice (for indeed the reader of *Corregidora* has to recognize that slavery must not ever be forgotten), her grandmother and great-grandmother burden Ursa by insisting on her reproductive responsibility to perpetuate the legacy of enslavement which is *theirs*—a responsibility which she cannot fulfill, although she tries.[9]

Ursa has known the details of her ancestors' enslavement to and abuse at the hands of Corregidora since she was a child; hoisted on her grandmother's knee, Ursa intuits the significance of what she is being told even if she is not mature enough to understand the facts themselves. More than the words, the memory of her grandmother's hands pressing on her thighs remains with Ursa, and reflecting on the oft-repeated story of the Portuguese seaman and the atrocities he perpetrated, Ursa thinks, "I was five years old then" (14). The simplicity of the statement, juxtaposed to the ornateness of the tale of subjugation, incest, and homosexuality, grants the reader a brief glimpse of Ursa's perspective as that five-year-old child on her grandmother's knee, and the horror of her burden becomes readily apparent.[10] The men with whom Ursa is involved recognize that the pain she suffers is not her own. Early in their relationship, Tadpole, to whom Ursa has told a bit of her history, articulates his view that Ursa's troubles—the nightmares she suffers and the profound ambivalence she feels towards Mutt and the loss of her ability to conceive—stem from the pressures invoked by her female relations. "Get their devils off your back. Not yours, *theirs*" (61), he tells her.

Failing to transcend the legacy of her female ancestors is perhaps Ursa's greatest personal flaw, and it becomes her greatest life challenge. Through the course of the narrative Ursa gradually recognizes that the struggle she has been engaged in is not her struggle, and that the loss of her womb, though traumatic and, indeed, tragic, need not be so for the reasons that she is feeling. Conditioned by her great-grandmother, her grandmother, and her mother, Ursa early on acknowledges, "Their past in my blood" (45), and states, "Always their memories, but never my own" (100). Her story is most certainly a woman in search of identity story *and* a woman as sex object story, not only from the moment when we enter the text—the moment Mutt pushes her down the steps at Happy's Cafe—but from the very beginning of her life. I would argue that the incident at Happy's is a fortuitous fall; in fact, Ursa describes it as a fall. The narrative perspective is interesting; although Ursa has already delineated Mutt's irrational jealousy and we recognize that he has pushed her down the back steps, Ursa seems to absorb the blame subconsciously as she narrates the event: "That was when I fell" (4). Clearly, her mother's warning not to "bruise any of [her] seeds" (41) overshadows Ursa's perceptions as she relates and relives the event, and the flat matter-of-factness of the statement causes it to stand apart from the rest of the text. The moment serves retrospectively as an avenue of insight for the reader into Ursa's character, just as the incident itself serves eventually as the fulcrum motivating Ursa's drive for self-recognition and self-acceptance.

At the end of Part II of the narrative, Ursa reflects on her visit with her mother and on the truth her mother has finally revealed—the stories of her relationship with her own mother and grandmother and of her brief marriage to Ursa's father. Perhaps it is motivational for Ursa to understand finally that her mother suffered similarly at the hands of the older Corregidora women. Falling asleep on the busride home, Ursa realizes that she has derived both comfort and a challenge from her visit. "I was thinking that now that Mama had gotten it all out, her own memory—at least to me anyway—maybe she and *some man*. . . . But then, I was thinking, what had I done about my *own* life?" (132)

Initially the reader knows very little about Ursa's relationship with her mother; the emphasis seems always to be on the older women who directly suffered Corregidora's abuse. We do know, however, that Ursa's mother disapproves of her singing. Although Ursa pursues singing in spite of her mother's objections, it is not until after her visit and the awareness that she herself has done nothing "about [her] own life" that she repositions her mother's emphasis on singing as destruction and instead turns to the blues as salvation. "They squeezed Corregidora into me, and I sung back in return" (103). In short, blues singing becomes for Ursa the new tradition—the tradition that for her replaces childbearing.

Although she does not immediately recognize its life-transforming potential, from the very first page of the narrative Ursa has acknowledged the importance of her singing: "It was something I had to do" (1). After the incident with Mutt the quality of her voice changes; Cat tells her, "Before it was beautiful too, but you sound like you been through more now" (44). Indeed, Ursa's accident and recovery process are the impetus for a new song.

The loss of her womb empowers Ursa to realize the essence of the blues; in singing out her experience, she takes the first step not only towards healing but also towards actual independence. Janice Harris maintains that Ursa's story is "an uncompromising portrait of the artist as a young woman" (2) but argues that once Ursa finds her song, "the fact that she sings that song and no other demonstrates the dependence within her independence" (3). However, Harris misses one key component of Ursa's discovery; while Corregidora is at the center of her maternal elders' stories,[11] Ursa places herself at the center of the blues narrative she finally creates.

Jones foreshadows the move Ursa finally makes in taking charge of her own life about halfway through the novel when Ursa relates a troubling dream, a dream that gives voice to the inclination she harbors to relegate Corregidora to the past in order to prioritize her own life. Sandwiched between memories of her relationship with Mutt and its unpleasant end and her present involvement with Tadpole, the dream manifests Ursa's deep-seated anxiety regarding the legacy of her enslaved past, her foremothers' injunction to "make generations," and the birth process itself.

I dreamed that my belly was swollen and restless, and I lay without moving, gave birth without struggle, without feeling. But my eyes never turned to my feet. I never saw what squatted between my knees. But I felt the humming and beating of wings and claws in my thighs. And I felt a stiff penis inside me. "Those who have fucked their daughters would not hes-

itate to fuck their own mothers." Who are you? Who have I born? His
hair was like white wings, and we were united at birth.
"Who are you?"
"You don't even know your own father?"
"You are not my father. I never was one of your women." (76–77)

The imagery at the beginning of the dream sequence is reminiscent of that found in Yeats' poem "Leda and the Swan," which depicts the rape of Leda by Zeus, who has assumed the form of a magnificent white bird.[12] The "white wings" of Corregidora's hair suggest the swan's "feathered glory" and the "humming and beating of wings and claws in [Ursa's] thighs" recall the graphic image of the body of the swan pressing against Leda's "loosening thighs" while her "terrified vague fingers" push against the obstacle, which is so much larger and greater than herself. So, too, Ursa fights Corregidora, even as she dreams of giving birth to him.

This passage is characteristic of the novel as a whole for the way in which it ambiguates Ursa's understanding of herself and her relationship with her white ancestor; in her adamant statement "I never was one of your women," the reader senses both protest and denial. However, if we interpret the entire narrative as Ursa's blues rendition of her life and her family's past, then the statement adopts new resonance—it becomes a statement of affirmation, a microcosm of the narrative itself. In singing her "new world song," Ursa combines love and hate, negotiating humanity's two most profound emotions. Aptly entitled "Corregidora" in acknowledgment of that part of her formative past, the song as Ursa finally sings it moves away from the patriarch and celebrates her newfound ability to create. Recognizing that she *can* generate something, Ursa bears witness[13] in a more constructive way by expiating the hurtful side of her history every time she raises her voice in song.

The reader cannot miss the additional emphasis on Ursa's singing as the narrative draws to a close. Most poignant, perhaps, is her encounter with the drunk patron at the Spider who compares her with Billie Holiday. The man seems to suggest that Ursa, although she only performs in a small club, evokes the same magic as the great blues singer. While this may be flattering to Ursa and testimony to the development of her talent, the scene shifts when the patron makes a vulgar remark, asking about Ursa's pussy. At once Jones reminds us of Ursa's unfortunate history with men, men who are kind and cruel simultaneously. This incident is different, however, as Ursa remains calm and in control, not relying on any outsider to assist her as she draws her conversation with the man to a close. Particularly significant is the fact that Ursa does not allow the encounter to disturb her; it brings with it no unpleasant flashbacks to her maternal ancestors or to her own previous relationships.

The incident with the drunken patron at the Spider, whose behavior might serve to remind us of Mutt's twenty-two years earlier, foreshadows Ursa's reunion with him. When Mutt arrives at the Spider, Ursa is prepared emotionally and strong physically. Although she tells Sal Cooper that she is unsure what her reaction will be when they meet again after all the years—"I won't know till I see him" (181)—her exchange with the previous Spider patron forecasts the changed woman she has become. And when she agrees to return to Mutt's room with him, we are as confident as Ursa is in her independence.

The act of fellatio Ursa performs comes as a surprise to Mutt, who remembers that throughout their first relationship Ursa would never participate in oral sex. Of course, Ursa does it not for him but for herself; just as she sings her own song, she performs this act of independence, an act she was not asked or commanded to do. In the gesture she merges finally[14] with her maternal ancestors, awakening to the awareness that what Great Gram did to Corregidora "had to be sexual" (184).

Performing fellatio on Mutt places Ursa in a new position of power, just as singing her "new world song" does. No longer is she the victim.[15] When she sings "Corregidora" she succeeds in objectifying the white slavemaster by forcing him to occupy a role as a character in *her* life drama, and she reverses the nexus of power in the sexual relationship she shares with Mutt by objectifying him, forcing him to submit to her sexual act. The call-and-response exchange she enters into with Mutt at the climax of their sexual encounter signals her acceptance of who she has become—a woman secure in her identity and responsive to her own sexuality, a woman who will make no promises to anyone other than herself.

"I don't want a kind of woman that hurt you," he said.
"Then you don't want me."

"I don't want a kind of woman that hurt you."

"Then you don't want me."

"I don't want a kind of woman that hurt you."

"Then you don't want me."

He shook me till I fell against him crying. "I don't want a kind of man that'll hurt me neither," I said. (185)

No longer will Ursa rely solely on her maternal ancestors' interpretation of who she is, no longer will she allow men to define and exploit, even enslave her. Instead, Ursa will nurture herself. Although the biological fact that she is unable to conceive a child is irreversible, Ursa finally fills that void in her life by giving birth to and nurturing the child within herself, the child whose cry is the blues song "Corregidora."

KINDRED: BIRTH OF THE OTHER

Gayl Jones was not the only black writer working in the 1970s to explicitly connect gender and slavery; Octavia Butler, the author of several critically acclaimed science fiction novels prior to 1979, took up the topic of American slavery and its impact on one twentieth-century black woman in her 1979 novel *Kindred.* In "Homage to Tradition: Octavia Butler Renovates the Historical Novel," Sandra Y. Govan argues that "Without turning to an actual slave narrative, there is probably no more vivid description of life on an Eastern Shore plantation than that found in *Kindred*" ("Homage" 94). Aside from Butler's choice to set the majority of her novel in antebellum Maryland, one striking difference distinguishes *Kindred* from *Corregidora.* Whereas Ursa is seemingly hyper-sensitive to the past, living most of her life in the shadow of her maternal ancestors and their experiences in slavery, Dana at the beginning of *Kindred* has virtually no historical awareness. This is perhaps best illustrated by the careless reference she makes to the temporary agency that employs her: "[W]e regulars called it a slave market" (52). Dana lives very much in the present; she is a 1970s working girl, struggling at a mindless day job in the hopes of one day becoming a successful writer.

But Butler intended to pen far more than an account of life in contemporary America when she began the project of writing *Kin-*

dred. The novel itself is a conglomeration of genres—historical fiction, slave narrative, and science fiction all meet and mingle, although Butler herself adamantly refers to the novel as "fantasy" (Kenan 495).[16] What is unique about *Kindred* is the melding of contemporary life and historical reality; Butler borrows liberally from the conventions of the nineteenth-century slave narrative, she infuses her work with the drama of this country's most controversial historical era, and she employs stock science fiction concepts of telekinesis and chronoportation—but devoid of any scientific explanation—to undergird her plot.[17] As Robert Crossley points out in his introduction to the 1988 Black Women Writers edition of the novel, "Inevitably, readers will wonder what provoked the author to adapt the form of a fantastic travelogue to a restoration of the genre of slave-memoir" (xii). The resulting novel, however, is brilliant both for the way that it explores slave life and master-slave relations in the antebellum South and problematizes our twentieth-century understanding of the peculiar institution.

More so even than Gayl Jones in *Corregidora*, who sought to demonstrate that her protagonist's womanhood was not merely something appropriated by men but was a vital and complex link both to her past and to her present as a black woman in twentieth-century America, Octavia Butler is concerned with the past. Just as Gayl Jones enabled Ursa to give birth to her true self by expiating her inner demons through her own original blues song, Butler illustrates the need for her protagonist to rejuvenate herself.[18] To do so, Dana must come to terms with herself and her heritage by facilitating the "birth" of the abusive white slaveholder who is her direct though distant ancestor; as she struggles to ensure that her family tree remains alive, Dana unknowingly facilitates her own spiritual and cultural birth as well.

On the day of her twenty-sixth birthday Dana discovers that her destiny is inextricably entangled with that of Rufus Weylin, who is four or five years old at the beginning of the novel. Although she does not understand the *how* of the situation, Dana quickly realizes that she is transported to the Weylin plantation in antebellum Maryland every time the young boy's life is in danger. The significance of their relationship dawns gradually on Dana when she realizes that Rufus Weylin is her great-grandfather, several times removed, and she intuits that her role is to save Rufus from life-threatening accidents so that he may survive long enough to father a child whose name Dana recalls dimly from a family Bible, a baby girl named Hagar who will begin the branch of Dana's immediate family tree.

Dana's realization is startling, not only to her but to the reader as well. "[I]f I wasn't completely out of my mind, if I wasn't in the middle of the most perfect hallucination I'd ever heard of, if the child before me was real and was telling the truth, maybe he was one of my ancestors" (28). And so, Butler establishes the unusual premise for the narrative. It is indeed an odd yoking— twentieth-century black woman and nineteenth-century white boy. Rufus is a small child the first few times that Dana rescues him; he does not understand the way that she dresses, nor can he comprehend the fact that she does not refer to him automatically as "Master" and that she is insulted when he calls her "nigger." What is very real to him, however, is the iron fist of his father, Tom Weylin, a man who routinely whips his son along with his slaves. The reader senses Rufus' genuine concern when he tells Dana that she must address him with respect: "You're supposed to. . . . You'll get into trouble if you don't, if Daddy hears you" (30). It is in part because of Tom Weylin's harsh treatment of his son that Dana pities Rufus and does not begrudge assistance when the frightened boy summons her across time. In fact, Dana's presence is necessary to nurture Rufus during his boyhood because both Mr. and Mrs. Weylin are ineffectual, unloving parents.

Like the writers of the neo-slave narratives after her, Octavia Butler is concerned with issues of gender, motherhood, and slavery, imaginatively yoking the concepts to explore the biological contradictions of enslaved motherhood while at the same time using them to highlight the dangerous spiritual and cultural condition of a twentieth-century character who has allowed herself to become far removed from her heritage. I wish to argue that during his early years Dana functions as a surrogate mother to Rufus, a role that ultimately allows her to give birth to herself and, more specifically, to the whole person she has become as a result of her experiences in antebellum Maryland.

Although Dana is not a biological mother, certain behaviors surface in her interaction with Rufus that highlight the role she will play during his formative years. For instance, very early in their second encounter, after she has learned his name, Dana begins to call him "Rufe," an affectionate nickname. Also, because she is already aware of his father's cruelty, having been a victim of it herself when Tom Weylin aimed his rifle at her after she pulled Rufus from the river at the time of their first meeting, she protects Rufus not only by extinguishing the draperies he has set on fire but by instructing him to finish burning the evidence in his fireplace grate and to ask his mother for replacement curtains before his father can observe the damage he has done.

That Dana recognizes maternal feelings[19] for Rufus may be surprising to the contemporary reader, but we must bear in mind that almost from the beginning of the narrative Dana realizes that Rufus is a direct relative of hers. Recalling the family Bible she thinks, "So many relatives that I had never known, would never know. . . . Was that why I was here? Not only to insure the survival of one accident-prone small boy, but to insure my family's survival, my own birth" (28–29). Acting as surrogate mother to Rufus is a life-giving proposition both for Rufus and for Dana. The time she spends as a black person living in antebellum Maryland affords Dana the opportunity to connect with her ancestors and thus to touch a part of her personal heritage that previously went unacknowledged and to assume an active role in the shaping and survival of her own family tree. As the mother-figure in the novel Dana bears two burdens: she must protect Rufus' life by serving as his guardian but, and more importantly, she must nurture herself, filling gaps in tradition in her historical consciousness that she comes to recognize only when she leaves the twentieth century.

Govan calls Dana "a woman very much of the present" and yet the person selected to be Rufus' "mentor and . . . his teacher" ("Homage" 88–89). Dana recognizes the enormity of her responsibility as well as the inappropriateness of it. Pondering the paradox she thinks, "I was the worst possible guardian for him—a black woman to watch over him in a society that considered blacks sub-human, and a woman to watch over him in a society that considered women perennial children. I would have all I could do to look after myself" (68). Octavia Butler's achievement is similar to Sherley Anne Williams' in *Dessa Rose*, a novel in which blacks subversively gain power over whites and women emerge as strong leaders capable of managing their own destinies. In *Kindred* Butler also prioritizes both womanhood and blackness by reversing the conventional equation and demonstrating her female protagonist's necessity in a world that actively campaigned to deny her every fundamental human right. But Dana assumes even more responsibility than Dessa does; whereas Dessa must struggle for her own survival and that of her baby, Dana fights not only to ensure personal survival but also to impact in some way the lives of the enslaved persons she meets on the Weylin plantation.

Dana embraces as her goal the task of molding Rufus Weylin into a *humane* slaveholder. She recognizes that a difficult, if not impossible, challenge confronts her; as her visits to antebellum Maryland become more frequent and longer she grows to appreciate the profound cultural differences separating the early decades of the 1800s and her own 1970s California. Certainly, even before Dana encounters Rufus she is aware of prejudice. Unable to secure a job, she joins the ranks of the "nonpeople" (53), those who do mindless temporary work for minimum wage. At the job where she meets Kevin Franklin, the white man who will become her husband, she is taunted by a fellow worker who refers to them as "chocolate and vanilla porn" (56), and a woman at Dana's employment agency frankly tells Dana that she and Kevin make " 'the weirdest-looking couple' she had ever seen" (57). Perhaps the most flagrant example of twentieth-century racism manifests itself in the reactions of Dana's and Kevin's families when they announce their intention to marry; both Dana's aunt and uncle and Kevin's sister are unwilling to accept the interracial union.

Nothing, however, prepares her for the almost instinctual hatred that victimizes anyone with dark skin in antebellum Maryland. Dana's mere presence provokes overt suspicion, even violence—on her second trip she is nearly raped by a patroller who returns in search of the mother of Alice Greenwood, Dana's distant ancestor; the case of mistaken identity does not foil the white man in search of a black woman to satisfy his sexual appetite. Dana's contact with Rufus' family is no different. The first time Rufus calls her to Maryland she immediately looks down the barrel of Tom Weylin's rifle; his lack of gratitude for her heroic, unquestioning deed is clearly symptomatic of his inherent racism. Tom Weylin distrusts Dana at once, in part because he does not understand her role in his family, but also because her sense of self-possession, her vocabulary, and her diction do not conform to what he believes about the black race.[20]

In part because Tom Weylin as a parent is such a poor role model for his son, Dana does more than merely rescue Rufus; she attempts to educate and nurture him. She cannot, of course, convey her book learning to Rufus; Tom Weylin can barely tolerate the fact that she knows how to read[21]—but when Kevin finds himself in antebellum Maryland with Dana he agrees to teach Rufus. Rufus is woefully behind other white children his age, and according to his father he is stupid, perhaps even retarded. Dana wishes for a more active role in educating the boy, especially since she witnesses firsthand how his father's ignorance influences his treatment both of his family and of his slaves. Kevin offers to assist Dana in attempting to educate Rufus. Arranging for Dana to read aloud to Rufus, Kevin enables her access to the child as well as precious time to relax and enjoy herself a bit. She reads from the classics— *Robinson Crusoe*, *Pilgrim's Progress*, and *Gulliver's Travels*— broadening Rufus' provincial knowledge of the world while simultaneously instructing him by the very example of her own life. Demonstrating that she can read well, making the words on the page come alive, Dana hopes to break Rufus' stereotype of "niggers"; by talking a bit about the relationship she and Kevin share, telling him, for instance, that they are married and that this is perfectly acceptable in their time, Dana attempts to make Rufus more progressive. Unfortunately, Dana's nurturing effects little change in Rufus' character.

The other force that Dana works to counterbalance is Margaret Weylin, who is as insufficient a parent and role model as her husband. Even as a young boy Rufus recognizes that his parents do not share a healthy, loving relationship; when Dana asks him if his mother will replace his burned draperies without his father's knowledge, Rufus replies, "I think so . . . [t]hey hardly talk to each other anyway" (32). Whereas Tom Weylin is stern, even cruel in his treatment of his child, Mrs. Weylin is an ineffectual, enervated woman who seeks to keep Rufus in a perpetual state of childhood. Doting on Rufus and tormenting the household slaves are the two activities that occupy her time.

Patricia Hill Collins, in her article "The Meaning of Motherhood in Black Culture and Black Mother/Daughter Relationships," begins by examining Eurocentric views of motherhood, views that particularly flourished in the South before the Civil War. According to Collins, "The cult of true womanhood, with its emphasis on motherhood as woman's highest calling, has long held a special place in the gender symbolism of white Americans. From this perspective, women's activities should be confined to the care of children, the nurturing of a husband, and the maintenance of the household" (3). Margaret Weylin fails even to conform to this definition; there is no evidence that she nurtures her husband, and blacks, including Dana, maintain the household with little supervision, but ample criticism, from her. Released from these obligations, Mrs. Weylin is free to devote all of her time to Rufus, smothering him with saccharine affection and sweets from the kitchen.

Margaret Weylin cares as little for Dana as her husband does, but her dislike does not seem to be racially motivated. Instead she manifests great fear, from the moment of Dana's first appearance, that someone other than herself will be able to do something for her child. When Dana drags Rufus to the shore after his near-drowning, Margaret immediately pummels her, accusing her of killing him. As Dana shoves her aside so that she can administer first aid, his mother collapses, overcome by the possibility of losing her child and unable to be of any assistance. Like her husband, she fails to thank Dana but turns all of her attention to Rufus once she realizes that he is safe.

Butler dramatizes Margaret Weylin's dislike for Dana more vividly in the incident when Rufus breaks his leg, making it clear to the reader that the woman's motherly instincts are misguided. Again Mrs. Weylin attacks Dana for hurting her child, and Dana thinks, "She had only one reaction when Rufus was in trouble. One wrong reaction" (69). She responds similarly to the doctor who sets Rufus' leg; Kevin shows Dana the bloody scratch-marks on his arms saying, "When she finished with me, she started on the doctor. 'Stop hurting my baby!' " (78). From these few examples it becomes readily apparent that Rufus Weylin is an extremely needy child, a child whose needs are fulfilled neither by his austere, cruel father nor by the overprotective mother who fails to discipline him. While they are his biological parents, they are parents in name only. It is Dana who attempts to fill the void in Rufus' life, serving each time she is called to Maryland as his primary physical, intellectual, and moral guardian.

The different approaches Dana and Margaret bring to Rufus' bedside as he is recovering from his broken leg, and his responses to them, further reinforce the hierarchy of maternal presence Butler is working to establish. When Margaret Weylin tells Rufus that Dana cannot read, her lie is exposed. He frequently begs for Dana's presence so that she can amuse him as he heals, while at the same time he grows tired and petulant in his mother's company. Furthermore, Rufus is disrespectful to his mother, harshly commanding her to leave him alone when she begins to annoy him with her insistent questions and offers and confident that although he has made her cry she will return shortly with a large piece of cake for him. Fittingly, Rufus justifies his actions towards his mother by citing his father's behavior: "Daddy does it too" (104); in fact, Rufus' behavior towards his mother predicts the type of person he will grow up to be.

Rarely, however, does Rufus treat Dana with disrespect, although the relationship they share changes as he grows older. Rufus still calls Dana when he needs to be rescued from danger, yet he has lost some of his childlike fascination with her. At the time of her third trip to Maryland, Rufus' neediness surfaces almost immediately. As Dana walks to a stream to wet her handkerchief he pleads with her to stay and assist him. "I could hear his increasing desperation. He was hurt and alone except for me" (122). Dana estimates that Rufus is now about eighteen or nineteen, and she is appalled to learn that he has raped Alice Greenwood. The type of bargaining they engage in speaks volumes about their changing roles. Dana still maintains some maternal influence over Rufus and his actions, convincing him, for instance, to say that white men attacked him rather than admit to the fight with Isaac, the enslaved man whom Dana hopes will get a head start running away with Alice. Yet this time, as she begins to pressure him into making the morally correct decision, Rufus snaps, "You threaten me, I'll threaten you. Without me, you'll never find Kevin" (125). This incident reveals the man that Rufus is becoming and foreshadows his final meeting with Dana, when he threatens her not with words but with physical and sexual violence.

Ultimately, Dana's efforts to mold Rufus into a humane slave-holder are undermined by familial and societal norms that are stronger and have a greater impact on shaping Rufus' day-to-day life.[22] Indeed, by the time of their final encounter Dana no longer functions as a surrogate mother to Rufus, although it is Rufus and not Dana herself who repositions her role in his life. Consumed by emotion at the loss of Alice, the young black girl whom he has made his mistress against her will and who has committed suicide after mistakenly believing that Rufus has sold their children, he reverts to his earlier childlike ways, weeping with Dana and agreeing almost blindly to her demand for certificates of freedom for the children. He seems genuinely pained by Dana's accusation that he may as well have killed Alice with his own hands, and responds much like a child who is receiving a severe scolding. However, in his grief he reaches out to Dana not as a mother but as a woman— something he has never done before—and his behavior is clearly inappropriate.

During her final encounter with Rufus, Dana faces the most difficult time she has experienced in Maryland. Because she has had a hand in Rufus' upbringing, she has an emotional attachment to him although she disapproves of some of his behavior. Dana learns, in a few short months, how difficult it is to be a mother, to watch a child deviate from what she has tried to teach. According to Govan in "Connections, Links, and Extended Networks: Patterns in Octavia Butler's Science Fiction," Dana discovers as much about herself as she does about Rufus as she witnesses the culmination of her efforts to raise that paradoxical creature, a humane slaveholder. "Try as she might, she is unable to teach the maturing Rufus enough about respect, responsibility, or compassion to prevent him from adopting the behavioral patterns of his class and race" (86). The nurturing Dana provides is not sufficient; without ever experiencing the biological aspect of motherhood, Dana comes to the same realization that all women who raise children inevitably do: after doing the best they can with their children, eventually the children are responsible for their own actions.

Butler prefaces Dana's showdown with Rufus early in the narrative. When the white patroller mistakes Dana for Alice's mother, whom he has returned to rape, Dana fears for her life but realizes that she can defend herself by injuring and possibly killing her attacker. Almost immediately after thinking of a way to save herself, however, Dana realizes that she cannot bring herself to harm another person. "My squeamishness belonged in another century, but I'd brought it along with me" (42). Finally, in a moment of desperation Dana ends the confrontation by stunning the man with a heavy tree limb, but not without regret. Dana risks being sold into slavery in order to spare another person's life, but on her return to present-day California she heeds Kevin's warning when he advises her to pack a knife for protection during future trips.

Although Dana hopes that she will never resort to the violence that the knife symbolizes to her, when Rufus approaches her on the subject of becoming his mistress and threatens to become violent if she does not agree, Dana's first thought is of her knife. Once Rufus lunges on top of Dana she has no choice other than to free herself of him by force. Yet still she is reluctant. "But it would be so hard to raise the knife, drive it into the flesh I had saved so many times. So hard to kill" (260). In this passage we see the remaining vestiges of Dana's maternal feelings for Rufus. How can a mother, surrogate or otherwise, kill the child she has nurtured?[23] The realities of what she has witnessed in slavery overcome Dana, however, and her decision is made. "A slave was a slave. Anything could be done to her. And Rufus was Rufus—erratic, alternately generous and vicious. I could accept him as my ancestor, my younger brother, my friend, but not as my master, and not as my lover. He had understood that once" (260). Tellingly, Dana repositions her relationship with Rufus at this crucial juncture; he is not the son she has assisted in raising but someone else—a relative, an acquaintance, a friend, but not a part of the maternal bond she has felt. Separating herself from the child to whom she has offered her love, her protection, and her wisdom, Dana sinks the knife into Rufus and succeeds in separating herself from the threat of slavery forever. "He screamed. I had never heard anyone scream that way—an animal sound. He screamed again, a low, ugly gurgle" (260). At the moment of Rufus' death Dana perceives him not as human but as animal, indicative, perhaps, that the final Rufus she sees is not the small, frightened boy but the cruel slaveholding man.

Morally, the decision to kill Rufus is not the only difficult choice Dana makes. She also serves, in a lesser capacity, as a mother figure to Alice Greenwood. Like Rufus, Alice is also a child when Dana is first called to Maryland, and Dana offers her comfort and protection when the white patrollers storm through her home looking for her father. This is the beginning of a friendship that is both trusting and questioning; Dana likes Alice in spite of her strong will, and Alice does not always understand the twentieth-century approach Dana brings with her to the Weylin plantation. When Alice is horribly beaten as punishment for running with Isaac, it is Dana who nurses her back to life, who teaches her gradually how to care for herself again, who tells her the truth about her new status as enslaved rather than free, and who comforts her when she begins to remember the details of her terrible ordeal. These examples all serve to illustrate the maternal interest Dana takes in Alice; in fact, at the time of this incident, Alice needs a mother-figure more than Rufus ever does.

As a young black woman in a hostile environment, Alice learns to become independent, a trait Rufus never develops due to his mother's smothering care and his father's indifference. As Alice grows older, Dana becomes more of a big-sister figure in her life, serving as a companion for long talks and advice. When Rufus attempts to coerce Dana into becoming his advocate with Alice, whom he is ready to take as his mistress, Dana understandably balks, aware of the double significance of what Rufus requests. Dana knows, although Alice does not, that Alice is destined to conceive Hagar, Dana's immediate ancestor, with Rufus, and in saving Rufus again and again Dana has tacitly acknowledged her role as facilitator. Yet abetting the sexual slavery of another woman goes against all that Dana believes, both from her twentieth-century perspective and from her newly acquired vantage point as a nineteenth-century enslaved person. Her attitude is clear—she calls it "rape" (162). Dana acquiesces, however, seeing the wisdom of trying to spare Alice some pain, when she realizes that Rufus will, in fact, rape Alice if she does not willingly oblige his desire. Rufus tries to convince Dana that her appeal to Alice will be a gesture of friendship, sisterhood even; although Dana vehemently disagrees, she follows through with Rufus' plan. "He had all the low cunning of his class. No, I couldn't refuse to help the girl—help her avoid at least some pain. But she wouldn't think much of me for helping her this way. I didn't think much of myself" (164).

Here Butler flirts with dangerous subject matter; magnifying the role gender plays in Dana's experiences in slavery, she complexifies her protagonist by holding her partially responsible for the sexual use and abuse of one of her sisters, the greatest violation black women suffered during slavery. Perhaps she positions Dana in this plight so that she can experience a bit of what *black* motherhood is like; in turning Alice over to Rufus, Dana is fully aware of his intentions and yet is helpless to protect the young woman whom she has nursed as her own child.[24] Furthermore, it is important to note that although Dana participates fully in the life of an enslaved person—she lives in primitive conditions, she is beaten, she is sent to work in the fields—she is never raped. Having such close access to Alice's plight engages Dana vicariously in some sharing of Alice's suffering without actually being violated herself.

Rufus verbalizes what the reader has intuited by the conclusion of the narrative when he states to Dana, "You're so much like her, I can hardly stand it. . . . You were one woman. . . . You and her. One woman. Two halves of a whole" (257). He uses this observation to justify his decision to possess Dana as his replacement mistress. Early in the narrative Butler takes pains to establish the women's physical similarities, and the two are temperamentally alike as well, both proud and strong-willed, and both able to challenge Rufus. But Rufus' statement serves as the thematic culmination of Butler's narrative; in making Dana and Alice "one woman. Two halves of a whole" Butler reinforces the close link between Dana and her maternal ancestor, the link that Dana discovers and that she gradually recognizes as vitally important to her own wholeness. As Govan describes the relationship between Dana and Alice, "It is as if the folk wisdom of 'there but for the grace of God go I' had suddenly become manifest" ("Homage" 93). Dana derives great strength from the example of her maternal ancestor; in fact, even Alice's suicide inspires Dana, giving her the courage not to submit to Rufus, a courage she takes with her upon her final return to her own time. While Dana was unable to "complete" Alice,[25] knowing Alice and sharing her experiences in slavery makes Dana a whole woman, a twentieth-century black woman in touch with her own painful personal history and with the past of all African Americans.

Beverly Friend, in "Time Travel as a Feminist Didactic in Works by Phyllis Eisenstein, Marlys Millhiser, and Octavia Butler," disagrees with this assessment, concluding that the works she examines, including *Kindred*, fail in their purpose. She argues that the feminist time travel novels she has studied illustrate that "contemporary woman is *not* educated to survive, that she is helpless, perhaps even more helpless, than her predecessors" (55, emphasis mine).[26] However, Friend completely misses the mark in her evaluation of *Kindred*. Making much of the injury Dana sustains when she returns to present-day California for the final time, Friend implies that Dana is not whole on her return, that the loss of her left arm symbolizes that part of herself she is forced to abandon to Rufus, the boy-turned-tyrant slaveholder. Friend further suggests that Dana returns emotionally crippled and unable to regain the threads of her contemporary life.

What Friend fails to take into consideration in this pessimistic feminist reading of *Kindred* is the fact that although Dana loses her arm, she gains something far more valuable. Travelling to Maryland with Kevin after she has healed, Dana's primary concern is for the enslaved men and women who were left on the plantation after Rufus' death. She finds records of the sale of many of them, a fact that saddens her deeply, and briefly questions why she ever wanted to return to the place where she had witnessed slavery—and slavery had touched her—firsthand. But Kevin reminds her that she came, with him, "To try to understand. To touch solid evidence that those people existed. To reassure yourself that you're sane" (264). From her experience Dana finally accomplishes the difficult task of individuating herself as a black woman in twentieth-century America, discovering a sense of personal history and developing a more intimate relationship with the black ancestors to whom she owes her existence. The process of rereading *Kindred* reveals the impact of the literal and the symbolic journey Dana has made; the very first line of the narrative, Dana's statement, "I lost an arm on my last trip home" (9), resonates with the ambiguity of the term "home," which now stands for both California and Maryland.

In her study of the fiction of Octavia Butler, Govan draws a conclusion that is particularly applicable to *Kindred*.

Each of Butler's heroines is a strong protagonist paired with, or matched against, an equally powerful male. This juxtaposition subtly illustrates differences in feminine/masculine values, differences in approaches to or conceptions of power, differences in the capacity to recognize and exercise social or personal responsibility. In each story, a physical, psychic, or attitudinal difference associated with the heroine sets her apart from society and often places her in jeopardy; each survives because her "difference" brings with it a greater faculty for constructive change. ("Connections" 84)

Dana's strength does indeed lie in her gender; she is intuitive, nurturing, and open, learning from the black women she encounters in the nineteenth century, including Alice but also Sarah, Carrie, Tess, and even Liza, the enslaved woman who reports Dana's escape attempt.[27] Although Dana is an unusual choice to mother— she has no children herself and her own parents are long dead— she excels in the patience, the self-sacrifice, and the love that the job demands. And along the way, Dana reaps rewards beyond what she might have imagined when she arrived for the first time on the muddy riverbank in antebellum Maryland.

Ursa Corregidora and Dana Franklin are similar heroines. Neither is a mother; in fact, neither woman has positive family ties to give her a sense of personal tradition. Both bury themselves in twentieth-century life, hoping to ignore the void they feel as a result of what they lack. And both suffer losses that prove to be life-giving. Whereas Ursa Corregidora loses her womb but subsequently gives birth to her true self, Dana forfeits her arm in the process of attempting to foster human decency in a small nineteenth-century white boy, and in the process of doing so she, like Ursa, gives birth to a new self. Both Ursa Corregidora and Dana Franklin are the great-granddaughters of Dessa, Sethe, and Always. According to Karen Elias-Button, "The process of reclaiming the mother involves, in part, an historical reaching-back to the lives women have lived before us, to find there the sense that our experience is rooted in a strength that has managed to survive the centuries" (201). Not biological mothers—perhaps even reluctant in their mothering—Ursa and Dana, when they reach across the centuries, find not merely their kin but also themselves. Gayl Jones and Octavia Butler, too, reach across time—backwards to find provocative, interesting and relevant subject matter to explore, and also forward, preparing the way for the neo-slave narratives that ultimately assure the enslaved woman a legitimate place in American history.

NOTES

1. Jones herself refers to the narrative as a "blues novel," stating that "the relationships between the men and women are blues relationships" (Rowell 48).

2. It must be acknowledged, however, that many readers are alienated both by the content and by the language of Jones' novels and that what I am celebrating as innovative others find offensive. Her 1976 novel *Eva's Man*, which shares themes with *Corregidora*, has come under particular attack; Michael G. Cooke, for instance, in "Recent Novels: Women Bearing Violence," calls that work "a heavily repetitive, possessed *female* fantasy that works as a vindictive counterpart to the male-controlled vagina dentata" (*Yale Review* 66 [Autumn 1976]: 150).

3. A distinction exists between Brazilian slavery and American slavery, particularly as it affected enslaved females. Sally Robinson, in her chapter " 'We're all consequences of something': Cultural Mythologies of Gender and Race in the Novels of Gayl Jones," in her *Engendering the Subject: Gender and Self-Representation in Contemporary Women's Fiction* (Albany: State University Press of New York, 1991), characterizes Brazilian slavemasters as more interested in using their female slaves as prostitutes— thus realizing direct economic profit—as opposed to breeders. She bases her conclusions on the work of Carl Degler in *Neither Black nor White: Slavery and Race Relations in Brazil and the United States* (New York: MacMillan, 1971).

4. There is some quality of liberation, of course, in echoing the language of her maternal ancestors and retelling their story; for Ursa, acknowledging her past is the first step in breaking free from the legacy.

5. Richard K. Barksdale makes this point in his article "Castration Symbolism in Recent Black American Fiction" (*CLAJ* 29:4 [June 1986]: 400–413), concluding that post-slavery black males, denied political and economic power, attempted to salvage their manhood by following the example of white masters who sexually victimized black women. He then utilizes this observation to disparage many contemporary black American

women writers, leveling the accusation that "the prototypical male cast-away can be found in abundant numbers on the pages of their fiction" (407).

6. Tadpole McCormick presents an interesting case of character inconsistency. Initially he conforms to the paradigm of gender-blurring I established in Chapter 3; when he cares for Ursa after her return from the hospital, he seems more female than male in his capacity to nurture and nourish. He prepares her first meal, he gives her his bed, he comes back to the room periodically to check on her, he turns the light out and closes the door when she is ready to sleep, he empties her bedpan and bathes her. All of these tasks are the same ones that mothers, and sometimes fathers, perform for their children. In fact, it could be argued that the diminutive of his name ("Taddy," which Ursa uses when she asks him to take her home from the hospital) sounds like "Daddy."

7. I am thinking, for instance, of the episode in which Mutt says to Ursa, "Your pussy's a little gold piece, ain't it, Urs? My little gold piece" (60).

8. Collins also quotes Gloria Wade-Gayles, who points out that the black mothers depicted in contemporary fiction by black women writers are "rarely affectionate" (8). This certainly describes Ursa's mother, grandmother, and great-grandmother, all of whom are foreboding presences whose intense stories trouble Ursa from a very early age.

9. It must be noted, however, that Ursa's ancestors' insistence on making their bodies bear witness is positive in that the act demonstrates their refusal to forget the horrors of enslavement. In some way Jones foreshadows what Morrison will do in *Beloved* with Sethe's scars.

10. Jones, in another way, implicates Ursa's female relations. The reader quickly notes that the only oral tradition handed down to each successive Corregidora woman is the story of Corregidora himself and his abuse of his slavewomen. In a culture that prides itself both on oral tradition and on the close bond between mothers and their daughters, the oversight on Jones's part is clearly intentional.

11. Robinson does an excellent job explicating the ways in which the Corregidora women are complicitous in perpetuating Corregidora's legacy of abuse.

12. It is interesting to note that Yeats himself was fascinated with the story of Leda and Zeus and interpreted Zeus' visit to Leda as an "annunciation" marking the beginning of Greek civilization. This anecdote usually accompanies the poem in a footnote. Perhaps Ursa's dream is meant to have an annunciatory quality as well—an articulation of what Ursa knows subconsciously ("I never was one of your women") but has been too timid to confront.

13. The symbolism of Ursa's name is crucial in establishing her as a survivor and adventurer. From the Latin "ursine" meaning "bear," her name accumulates layers of signification: she is unable to bear children; it becomes her personal trial to bear (endure) the legacy of slavery that is not fully hers and that she does not fully understand; and finally, she bears witness in her own important way, thus keeping alive the healthy aspect of her foremothers' imperative.

14. The language Jones uses is explicit: "It was like I didn't know how much was me and Mutt and how much was Great Gram and Corregidora" (184).

15. Jerry Ward, in "Escape from Trublem: The Fiction of Gayl Jones" (*Callaloo* 5:3 [1982]: 95–104), argues that Ursa's act at the end of the novel is "vindictive"; that is, she finally assumes "power" by making Mutt her victim. However, although Mutt is clearly in a submissive position as Ursa performs fellatio, it is important to keep in mind that the act of oral sex was something he desired at a previous point in their relationship. Furthermore, as in Williams' *Dessa Rose*, the reversal of power is, ultimately, the greater good.

16. When pressed by Kenan to categorize her work, Butler responded, "I don't like the labels, they're marketing tools . . . *Kindred* is fantasy. I mean literally, it is fantasy. There's no science in *Kindred*" (Kenan 495).

17. Govan, in her article "Homage to Tradition: Octavia Butler Renovates the Historical Novel" (*Melus* 13 [Spring/Summer 1986]: 79–96), discusses Butler's genre innovation, paying close attention to the ways in which Butler signifies on the slave narrative tradition, of particular relevance to my project here.

18. Interestingly, I could not find the name "Edana" (Dana's given name) in several name books I consulted. The closest name to it seems to be Edna which, from the Hebrew, means "rejuvenation."

19. I should note, however, that the first time Dana acts to save Rufus she is operating on human, as opposed to maternal, instinct; the text makes it clear that although she is not cognizant of how she got to the riverbank, she reacts immediately and without thought when she notices the young boy drowning. It is only when Dana becomes aware of the blood relationship she and Rufus share across the centuries that a more maternal urge to protect him, and thus to protect her black ancestors, develops.

20. Interestingly, when Kevin accidently accompanies Dana on her third trip to Maryland, Weylin interprets their relationship according to his own understanding of race relations during slavery and never thinks to question his conclusion. His easy acceptance of their sexual relationship

signals another form of prejudice; he appreciates and even condones the white man's sexual appetite for the black slave, even to the extent of acknowledging that it occurs under the roof of his seemingly Christian home.

21. Although it annoys Weylin that Dana can read, he uses the fact to goad his son. "You ought to be ashamed of yourself! A nigger can read better than you!" (102). This type of remark serves as a measure of exactly what type of person, and parent, Tom Weylin is.

22. Perhaps this is because Dana's presence in his life has only been sporadic—six visits of varying lengths over the twenty-five years of Rufus' life. However, one cannot overlook the fact that Dana's goal—to mold a *humane* slaveholder—was idealistic and, in fact, riddled with contradiction.

23. Both Toni Morrison in *Beloved* and J. California Cooper in *Family* explore the ramifications of this question and, like Octavia Butler, come to no easy conclusion.

24. Again, Butler foreshadows the work of black women writers working ten years later, who explore more fully the contradictions inherent to enslaved motherhood.

25. While it is not precisely "failure," Dana does not succeed in her relationship with either Rufus or Alice. Perhaps the cultural and time discrepancies forbid her from ever having the life-altering effect she hoped to have on both of them.

26. I am not familiar enough with the other writers Friend discusses to evaluate the accuracy of her conclusion as it applies to any works other than *Kindred*.

27. Dana's interaction with Sarah is particularly meaningful to her development. Initially she thinks of Sarah, "She had done the safe thing— had accepted a life in slavery because she was afraid. She was the type of woman who might have been called 'mammy' in some other household. She was the kind of woman who would be held in contempt during the militant nineteen sixties. The house-nigger, the handkerchief-head, the female Uncle Tom—the frightened powerless woman who had already lost all she could stand to lose, and who knew as little about the freedom of the North as she knew about the hereafter" (145). However, Dana mitigates her harsh appraisal of Sarah as she grows to learn more about Sarah's personal experiences in slavery and as she, herself, comes to understand the institution from an insider's point of view. Sarah becomes for Dana another model of black motherhood. Butler acknowledges her overtly didactic purpose for creating the character of Sarah when she

states, "*Kindred* was a kind of reaction to some of the things going on during the sixties when people were feeling ashamed of, or more strongly, angry with their parents for not having improved things faster" (Kenan 496), a point she elaborates on further in her interview with *The Black Scholar* (17:2 [March/April 1986]: 14–18).

6

"Children of Those Who Chose to Survive": Neo-Slave Narrative Authors Create Women of Resistance

What the authors of the works I have analyzed have in common is a keen interest in America's slave past and an insistence on placing strong female characters who mother at the center of their imaginative investigations into that past. In the previous chapters I have explored strategies that contemporary African American women writers have employed in reclaiming the slave narrative as genre. They do so, I argue, to reposition American written history to ensure proper recognition of the enslaved woman as a vivid and viable figure who contributed significantly to the communities of which she was a member, including, and perhaps most importantly, the enslaved black family. That slavery has become a popular topic for late-twentieth-century African American writers of both genders cannot be disputed; the past, always a rich source of subject matter for black artists, has recently presented itself in a new way—as an urgent, enigmatic puzzle holding tantalizing clues to identity for a people to whom self-definition has become increasingly important.

What remains for me to speculate upon is, first, the impact of contemporary African American writers, especially black women writers, who are breaking the silence that has previously characterized black literature with regard to the subject of slavery and, second, of the neo-slave narrative itself. In particular, I would like to address three questions: What contribution have late-twentieth-century black women writers made to the overall literary achievement of black women writers? What place does the neo-slave narrative occupy in the oeuvre of twentieth-century American literature? And, how does the perspective of the mother change our overall understanding of slavery and its impact on contemporary African American society?

In "Trajectories of Self-Definition: Placing Contemporary Afro-American Women's Fiction," Barbara Christian asserts that, "The extent to which Afro-American women writers in the seventies and eighties have been able to make a commitment to an exploration of self, as central rather than marginal, is a tribute to the insights they have culled in a century or so of literary activity" (172). Christian's essay is definitive in tracing the development of a tradition unique to black women writers, and it might be argued that there exists no finer treatment of black women's literature as a body of work.

Beginning with a brief examination of early novels such as *Iola Leroy* (Frances Harper, 1892) and *Contending Forces* (Pauline Hopkins, 1900), Christian illustrates her contention that the primary impetus these writers and their contemporaries felt was to challenge negative stereotypes of black women rather than to understand themselves (and their characters) as women. This tendency to concentrate on creating almost unrealistically positive images of black female characters persisted through the 1940s, although Zora Neale Hurston's *Their Eyes Were Watching God* (1937) and Ann Petry's *The Street* (1946) may be regarded as exceptions.

Christian identifies the publication of Gwendolyn Brooks' *Maud Martha* (1953) as a significant achievement in African American women's fiction. She celebrates that novel as the first in which a black female author depicts a female character living an ordinary life; "[w]hat Brooks emphasizes in the novel is Maud Martha's *awareness* that she is seen as common (and therefore unimportant), and that there is so much more in her than her 'little life' will allow her to be" (176). Perhaps most directly influenced by *Maud Martha* is Paule Marshall's *Brown Girl, Brownstones* (1959), significant for its thoughtful presentation of a black woman as mother and for its sensitive portrayal of the intricacies of black mother-daughter relationships. Together these works may be viewed as being in the forefront of a new movement aimed at defining the black woman in her own right, a challenge black women novelists writing in the 1970s, the 1980s, and the 1990s fully embraced.

One work that Christian neglects to mention in her overview is Margaret Walker's *Jubilee* (1966), arguing instead that black writers were focusing their energies during the 1960s on poetry and drama.[1] In Chapter 1 I discussed *Jubilee* as an invaluable work linking contemporary novels and the American slave narrative tradition. Walker places history at the center of her narrative, thus often obscuring the personal story of her foremother that she set out to write. It is an odd irony—Walker in 1966 published a novel inspired by and fairly accurate in its depiction of her own family's history in America, yet the work itself retains the flavor of stock historical novels, epic in scope and inevitable in its personification of the heroine as having universal significance. In spite of the novel's shortcomings, Walker must be acknowledged for the contribution she made to black women's literature—namely, the imagining of an enslaved female as speaking subject.

Having prepared for her analysis of contemporary black women writers, Christian differentiates between the literature produced in the 1970s and that produced in the early years of the 1980s, the time of Christian's writing. She asserts that as writers began to explore the themes of self-definition and female empowerment they targeted black-perpetuated racism and sexism, suggesting that reform must begin from within the community, and that that reform would have a direct impact upon the quality of life black women were experiencing. Novels such as *The Bluest Eye* (Toni Morrison, 1970), *Corregidora* (Gayl Jones, 1975) and *The Salt Eaters* (Toni Cade Bambara, 1980) illustrate black women writers' increasing concern with self-love, survival, and women's community, all themes that were previously unexplored but that beckoned invitingly, for they appeared to hold forth the promise of both personal and political change.

Even an analysis of the development of black women's writing as a body of work as careful as Barbara Christian's does not anticipate the gusto with which black women writers, as they moved into the 1980s, embraced these themes. For reasons that may perhaps never be fully explained, American audiences began to heed the works that were being produced. Alice Walker's *The Color Purple* (1982) received unprecedented attention and admiration, winning the American Book Award and the Pulitzer Prize for Fiction and selling over one million copies. Additionally, the novel, with its epistolary form and heavy reliance on rural folk speech to tell the story of black sharecroppers, became an immediate box-office success when it was released as a film in 1985 and garnered eleven Oscar nominations; it became the most talked-about, controversial film of the 1985–86 season for the issues it brought before the American people.

Perhaps most significant about *The Color Purple* and works that followed it is the fact that they begin to explore the black woman's past as the source of her future. Over the course of the narrative, Celie must come to know herself by uncovering, acknowledging, and coming to terms with her past, which includes her growing knowledge of Africa[2] and the twofold reconciliation she experiences—with the children she was forced to give up and with her own creative side. The novel ends with Celie's family reunion on the Fourth of July, Africans and African Americans celebrating together the privilege they share of being related and knowing each other. "Matter of fact, I think this the youngest us ever felt" (251), concludes Celie, testimony to the fact that by discovering the past and her own identity within the larger community Celie has finally empowered herself to begin the process of living.

Paule Marshall's *Praisesong for the Widow* (1983) and Gloria Naylor's *Mama Day* (1988) are two other recent novels that indicate black women writers' growing awareness of the past as vital to their characters' development. Marshall's protagonist, Avey Johnson, flees the luxurious cruiseship on which she has been vacationing and finds herself in an unanticipated search for her heritage on the tiny island of Carriacou. There she remembers her great-aunt Cuney's tales of the African Ibos brought in chains to the New World as well as Cuney's admonition never to forget her given name, Avatara. After participating in the Beg Pardon ceremony Avey renews her relationship with herself and her past and returns to the United States determined to live her past honorably by educating others, hoping to touch at least a few lives as her own has been touched.

Likewise, Gloria Naylor creates in *Mama Day* a world removed from materialistic twentieth-century American society in which to place her protagonist. Naylor is particularly careful to establish an entire mythology rooted in African tradition to govern Willow Springs and to imagine a strong female presence, in the figure of Mama Day, at the center of that world. Like Marshall, Naylor also alludes to slavery's defining influence (and the transcendence of that influence) on the territory, and she reinforces her theme of the importance of tradition by creating a collective black voice encompassing the past, the present, and the future to narrate much of her story. What both of these novels share is the removal of their protagonists from the mainstream of American life to a place more remote and more connected to an Afrocentric past, a place where the protagonists can get in touch with sides of themselves they have long forgotten or repressed.

Gwendolyn Brooks' attempt to imbue Maud Martha's "little life" with significance directly inspired these works and many others. With *The Color Purple* a distinct pattern begins to take shape; we see a conscious bridging of past and future, a development reflected in protagonists who are more open to a range of experiences, experiences that ultimately allow them to assume power over their own lives. As the literature has developed, those experiences may result from political involvement, from nurturing and healing, even from lesbian relationships and acts of violence. What matters is that black female characters are finally empowering themselves to choose the direction of their lives, and for many of them the key to this lies in reclaiming a past. Emerging from the literature of the 1970s and particularly of the 1980s and 1990s is a direct connection between awareness of and connectedness with the past and self-knowledge, that which invests everyday life with meaning. These characteristics culminate in the neo-slave narratives and afford the works wide-reaching significance.

According to Patricia Hill Collins in *Black Feminist Thought: Knowledge, Consciousness, and the Politics of Empowerment*, "Reclaiming the Black women's intellectual tradition involves examining the everyday ideas of Black women not previously considered intellectuals" (15). One excellent source for this project, as I have demonstrated, is the enslaved mother. Even a random perusal of contemporary neo-slave narratives reveals that their creators are not interested in writing in the tradition of Harper's *Iola Leroy*, about light-skinned heroines of impeccable moral stature; nor are these the women whom contemporary writers and their characters seek when looking backwards for inspiration in the search for identity and heritage.[3] Instead, these authors work like archeologists, attempting to uncover the secrets of the past, sometimes to instruct heroines who are confused about their present and unsure of their future, as in *Corregidora* and *Kindred*, other times to offer to today's readers more accurate models from which to draw strength and inspiration. It is a cooperative venture; today's black women writers are largely successful because they have formed a community characterized by conversation for and about the ordinary black woman[4]; while we cannot pinpoint a precise date for the genesis of the conversation, its focus is readily apparent—to respond to, to question, to probe, and to further each other's work in shared efforts to reclaim and celebrate the "everyday ideas" and actions of black women, perhaps the longest-neglected and most misrepresented Americans of all.

The literature produced in recent decades as a result of the conversation among contemporary black women writers has contributed to the expansion and reshaping of the American literary canon, about which there has been much discussion recently. As faculty seek to make their curricula more multicultural in an effort to reflect changing perceptions of what it means to be American and to have a national literature, works by women writers of all races have become increasingly valued. Voices long silent or silenced are now regularly included in surveys of American literature, and individuals who read for pleasure now find at local bookstores greater diversity of reading material.

Interest in greater historical accuracy is also on the rise, and in Chapter 1 I addressed revisionary historical scholarship as contributing to increased awareness of and tolerance for alternative perspectives on the American landscape. No longer is history narrated solely from the point of view of the white male. Complementing the efforts scholars of American history are making are works of literature by authors who adopt as their primary subject matter the past; they, too, are scholars of American history. The revival of the slave narrative as genre, freed from its rigid nineteenth-century conventions and its obligation to flatter white audiences, is the most significant development in late-twentieth-century American literature. Imaginative in ways its predecessors could not possibly be and yet factual in content and faithful to the spirit of the original slave narratives, the neo-slave narrative is responsible for adding a new voice into American literary discourse.

Although not referring to slavery specifically, Alice Walker has said that what she finds most interesting about American literature is "the way black writers and white writers seem . . . to be writing one immense story—the same story for the most part—with different parts of this immense story coming from a multitude of different perspectives. Until this is generally recognized, literature will always be broken into bits, black and white" (*In Search* 5). Prior to the emergence of the neo-slave narrative, the "immense story" that is American gave no voice to an entire segment of the population. Revisionist historians as well as civil rights activists and women's rights activists, all of whom gained prominence in the 1960s, are in great measure responsible for broaching the question of slavery's impact on the formation of America. The groundbreaking work of each of these groups prepared the way for the imaginative recreations later undertaken by black writers.

But why contemporary black *women* in particular became interested in America's slave past as a rich source of subject matter remains unanswered. As historians such as Angela Davis, Jacqueline Jones, and Deborah Gray White began to piece together definitive portraits of the lives of enslaved women, writers working creatively were complementing their revisionary scholarship. I would like to suggest, however, that in addition to the development of a community of African American women actively engaged in searching out their maternal ancestors, two other events are responsible for renewed interest in the slave narrative, interest so great that it has engendered an entirely new genre within American literature.

Nineteen hundred and seventy-six was the year which Americans devoted to celebrating freedom. Our nation's Bicentennial, commemorating two hundred years of independence from England, was perhaps the epitome of the America-as-melting-pot mentality. It did not seem to matter where a person's ancestors had sailed from; what mattered in 1976 was the fact of American citizenship and its accompanying freedom. However, it is understandable that black Americans may have felt a lesser part of the celebration, having been "free" for only one hundred years, and for much of that time only nominally so. The civil rights movement of the 1960s, which sought to overturn "separate but equal" in favor of wholly equal treatment for African Americans, had been successful, but its success was only gradually being realized. Indeed, the consciousness-raising efforts of the Black Power movement often seemed more tangible to blacks than the social and political reforms achieved as a result of sixties' activism. For many blacks, the celebration of America as truly their own country was an empty one.

Coinciding with America's Bicentennial was the pinnacle of one man's literary achievement, a birthday gift of sorts, that resonated with significance for many Americans, black and white. That work is Alex Haley's *Roots*. Published serially in 1974 in *Reader's Digest* and then as a novel in 1976, Haley's novel aired as a made-for-television miniseries in January, 1977. The chicken-and-egg question is easily answered in the case of *Roots*; the book, which graced best-sellers' lists for months and sold more than one million copies in 1977 alone, swept into vogue on the coattails of the miniseries, and thus *Roots* cannot be considered merely a literary phenomenon. Television critics estimated that approximately 130 million Americans watched at least part of the eight-day series, with 80 million viewers tuning in for the last episode. In a matter of one week, millions of Americans became fascinated with genealogy, as people of all ethnicities began the search for their own "roots."[5]

According to Haley, *Roots* was not directed solely at a black audience. When asked to account for the enormous success of both the television miniseries and the novel, Haley responded that his work touched "some deep pulse that transcends racial things" and that *Roots* seemed "to hold out a particular hope that they [Americans] could fill in their own blanks, repair the broken continuity of their history" (Gelman 30). Clearly, he pinpointed something deep in the collective American consciousness as he pursued his personal interest in his family's African heritage. But the work was especially meaningful for blacks; many saw it as the first open acknowledgment of the brutality of slavery. What was perhaps even more fulfilling than the fact that a work like *Roots* finally reached production was the enormous audience it drew, a signal to blacks that white America was responsive to the message of *Roots*—that Africans forced from their homeland and stripped of their culture were nevertheless people of dignity, people capable of incredible endurance, courage, and love.

Perhaps the time was right in the mid-1970s for such a message. Unquestionably, the Bicentennial had evoked tremendous feelings of national pride, and *Roots* provided something of a reality check, reminding Americans that much of what this country has become directly resulted from the enslaved labor of the African people. Also at this time the American public was coming to terms with the legacy of the Vietnam War, recognizing that a terrible mistake had been made, and perhaps even acknowledging that, in spite of the wave of patriotism and melting-pot idealism fostered by Bicentennial celebrations, the country did have its share of blemishes; the realities of America's slave past, as exposed by Alex Haley, loomed large among them.

In spite of the fanfare both the novel and the miniseries received, Haley's work did not escape scrutiny and criticism. Russell L. Adams, in his article entitled "An Analysis of the *Roots* Phenomenon in the Context of American Racial Conservatism," argues that "*Roots* touches the sentiments but fails to stretch the mind" (132) and also accuses Haley of presenting an overly romanticized, nostalgic view of the past. Although he praises the work as groundbreaking, Adams makes much of Haley's style, which he evaluates as simplistic yet calculating, developed as a result of years of writing for popular magazines. Likewise, in "Haley's *Roots* and Our Own: An Inquiry into the Nature of a Popular Phenomenon," David Gerber exposes flaws in Haley's work, although his focus tends to be on inconsistencies and factual inaccuracies within the narrative.

It is my contention that many black women writers also noted tremendous shortcomings in Haley's work, especially in the areas of gender representation and relations. From their perspective, Haley addressed the topics of African family life and African American slavery and its aftermath incompletely, neglecting to tell the whole story. Although it is not my intention here to provide a close analysis of *Roots* as a whole, it is obvious from the opening pages of the novel that Haley's purpose is to tell the story of village life, enslavement, and freedom from a male point of view.

The narrative begins with the birth of a "manchild" (11), Kunte Kinte, the distant relative who becomes for Haley the starting point of his saga. The opening chapter outlines the naming and dedication rituals that accompany the birth of a male child in Haley's ancestral village of Juffure, and Haley immediately establishes a tone of great pride. Binta, Kunta's mother, remains a shadowy figure, only significant for her role as childbearer. The irony is immediately apparent—during American slavery, an African woman was valued only for her ability to breed and thus to increase her owner's wealth. Haley does nothing to dignify Binta's role; she gives birth and returns to her job in the field. The only definitive action we observe Binta taking in the opening pages of the narrative is her decision to wean Kunta at an early age. However, she does so not for her own needs or for the needs of her child but to please her husband.

Subtitled "The Saga of an American Family," Haley's "evocation of slave family and kinship is the strongest claim which *Roots* has to the attention of a critical audience" (Gerber 94). However, Haley's lack of interest in the dynamics of African family life is obvious, and the tale quickly becomes Kunta Kinte's alone. We witness his boyhood, his abduction by slavecatchers, the perilous Middle Passage, and the establishment of his life enslaved in America, including his eventual marriage to Bell and the birth of their daughter Kizzy, who is sold away from the family when she is fifteen. In the tradition of Frederick Douglass' portrayal of himself, Haley portrays Kunta Kinte as a loner, enraged by his treatment at the hands of the toubob (his word for whites), determined to save himself, and willing to compromise with his fellow captives only if it means securing his own freedom.

Critics interested in how the novel depicts the American family under the yoke of slavery—previously unexplored subject matter in American literature—cannot help but be disappointed by Haley's lopsided emphasis on the male experience of slavery. Although *Roots* dramatizes and supports Herbert Gutman's scholarly contention that enslaved African Americans were able to and very often did form strong nuclear families,[6] Haley's lack of attention to the role of women in these families is notable. Kizzy is the most well-developed female character in the epic narrative. In the violation she suffers at the hands of Tom Lea, the white man who buys her, in her spirit of endurance and survival, and in the eventual community-building she enjoys with the other enslaved men and women, Kizzy prefigures the enslaved mothers I have examined in this work. As Gerber points out, "it seems almost as if Afro-America's roots begin with her rather than her father" (103). Yet Haley's overall treatment of Kizzy is problematic; he never allows her character to develop beyond the stock conventions of the suffering enslaved woman. Ultimately, she functions in the narrative only as George's mother, never as a person in her own right. Following the pattern he established in the opening chapter in delineating the Binta/Kunta relationship, Haley overtly chooses to prioritize George's story at the expense of Kizzy's.

This glaring oversight may have provided inspiration for contemporary black women writers. The tremendous success of *Roots*—both book and miniseries—signalled that Americans were, indeed, interested in the past and were amenable to previously neglected viewpoints. While Alex Haley may be perceived as a pioneer for the way in which he prepared the American public for slavery as a literary topic, black women writers are the true pioneers, giving voice to previously untold stories and in the process revising both historical assumptions about black women during slavery and popular conceptions of black women today. Their oppression becomes more real through the pages of the neo-slave narratives, but so, too, does their courage. If a literature truly is to be the representation of its people, then American literature can be no true representation without the voice of the enslaved black female contributing to the conversation about what it means to be an American. Her view—sad, marginalized, strong, triumphant—reflects her share in the human experience, yet has gone unrecognized since the founding of this country. The recognition and reclamation of this underappreciated voice is one of the most powerful developments in contemporary American literature, making the literature more resonant, more diverse and more thought-provoking, while at the same time providing new stories that are incredibly rich in entertainment value.

To be an enslaved woman meant almost inevitably to be an enslaved mother, and these stories are among the most moving to emerge from post-1960s revisionist scholarship. The contradictions—biological, social, and legal—inherent in being an enslaved mother offer an excellent starting point for contemporary black women writers, who began, with the neo-slave narrative, to problematize both slavery and motherhood by juxtaposing the two. As Angela Y. Davis points out in *Women, Race and Class*, "[Enslaved] women . . . were driven to defend their children by their passionate abhorrence of slavery. The source of their strength was not some mystical power attached to motherhood, but rather their concrete experiences as slaves" (29). Sethe, in *Beloved*, articulates most clearly the unique plight of the enslaved mother when she describes her relationship with her children after her escape from slavery:

It was a kind of selfishness I never knew nothing about before. It felt good. Good and right. I was big, Paul D, and deep and wide and when I stretched out my arms all my children could get in between. I was *that* wide. Look like I loved em more after I got here. Or maybe I couldn't love em proper in Kentucky because they wasn't mine to love. But when I got here, when I jumped down off that wagon—there wasn't nobody in the world I couldn't love if I wanted to. You know what I mean? (162)

"They wasn't mine to love"—Sethe's keen perception of her role in her children's lives under the confines of slavery emphasizes her awareness of herself, in society's eyes, as nothing more than a breeder for the white master. According to Elizabeth Fox-Genovese, when social conditions are unstable, gender may "come unstuck" from sexuality and gender confusion may result for both men and women (187).[7] This problem was magnified for enslaved persons, because slavery denied men the right to define themselves in the eyes of society as men, husbands, and fathers. As a result, enslaved women were unable to look to black men to form a satisfactory social identity for themselves as women (188). Instead, white males defined them as breeders, an identity that insisted on their reproductive capabilities but denied their status as social beings.

The women who are now choosing to write neo-slave narratives seem both fascinated and appalled by this dehumanization; their outrage is reflected in works that are designed not merely to reclaim their enslaved maternal ancestors' stories and reposition their role in American history, but also to refute the stereotype of the enslaved woman as breeder by resharpening the focus on her gender. Williams', Morrison's, and Cooper's success in portraying the enslaved mother as fully human links them with the earliest African American women writers who consciously sought to eradicate nineteenth-century stereotypes of black women. "Portraying African American women as stereotypical mammies, matriarchs, welfare recipients, and hot mammas has been essential to the political economy of domination fostering Black women's oppression. Challenging these controlling images has long been a core theme in Black feminist thought" (Collins *Black Feminist Thought* 67). That goal is especially relevant today.

The significance of the American neo-slave narrative is not merely literary. I have argued that the voice of the enslaved woman contributes in an important way to broadening and enhancing the American literary canon, but the project to reclaim the enslaved woman's stories has ramifications that extend to popular culture as well. In the view of Barbara Ransby and Tracye Matthews, who co-authored the article "Black Popular Culture and the Transcendence of Patriarchal Illusions," much of black popular culture is concerned with dilemmas specific to being a black male in today's society, and both the means of expressing those problems and the "pseudo-solutions" offered "further marginalise and denigrate Black women" (57). In particular, Ransby and Matthews analyze three phenomena of popular culture: the growing popularity of cultural and intellectual Afrocentrism, which they argue glorifies an African past unsuitable to the demands of today's society; the revival of interest in Malcolm X and other black prophet-heroes, whom they assert are blindly accepted by today's youth as role models in spite of the skewed message such hero worship sends that "only larger than life great men can make or change history" (62); and rap music, which they villify for its suggestions of sexual promiscuity, female objectification, and violent behavior. By focusing on black women in their narratives, contemporary African American women writers not only celebrate the black woman as she is today but articulate for their readers her rich and varied heritage, a heritage deserving of recognition and proud acknowledgment.

Many might argue that there is no better time to be a black woman in America than today. Indeed, the early years of the 1990s brought with them a burst of pride in Afrocentric culture. Afrocentrism[8] has manifested itself in fashion; it is common to see African Americans wearing tee-shirts honoring black women and celebrating their ties to Africa, and once again clothing and accessories made of kente cloth are popular. Oprah Winfrey was first on the list of *Forbes* magazine's forty top earning entertainers in 1993; that year she was worth $250 million, earning $5,416 for every minute she appeared on television (Bly 375); in 1995 she again topped the list. By 1997, estimates placed her worth at almost a half a billion dollars (M. Johnson 47). Audiences around the world widely recognize her—her show airs in sixty-four countries and is seen by almost 20 million viewers daily—and she addresses topics of particular interest to women and minorities. She is one of the country's most prominent role models for young African Americans. African American studies programs are increasing in popularity at colleges and universities across the country, and most bookstores now include well-stocked African American studies sections. And Zebra, a medium-sized publishing company, has inaugurated a line of romance novels featuring ethnic characters and storylines. After market research showed that one third of all romance novel readers are nonwhite, Zebra took a chance at targeting minority audiences, and the first two titles, both by black authors and featuring black characters, were immediately successful, attracting both white and minority readers (E. Updike 3E).

Additionally, the black woman's voice now contributes to the conversation that is rap music, once the exclusive domain of black male artists.[9] Many female rappers currently enjoying success choose to rap about women's issues, including sexism within the black community and the need for U-N-I-T-Y, the title of an enormously popular song by artist Queen Latifah. Some male rappers now celebrate, rather than disrespect, the black woman. For example, artist Heavy D's song "Black Coffee" is a tribute to the dark-skinned black woman, and as such repositions the common assumption that black men favor light-skinned women.

But for all the ways contemporary society affirms the black woman—affirms her strength, her beauty, her ability to succeed—negative images persist. Stuart Hall, in an article entitled "What Is This 'Black' in Black Popular Culture?," argues that "black popular culture is a contradictory space. It is a site of strategic contestation" (108). At the center of this tug of war stands the black mother. The arena where this is most obvious is the film industry. John Singleton and Spike Lee have achieved tremendous box-office success with films depicting contemporary urban African American life; Lee's *X*, the dramatization of the life of black revolutionary Malcolm X, touched off a wave of "Malcolmania" and introduced the black revolutionary to a generation of moviegoers who had not yet been born when Malcolm was at the height of his power in the 1960s. And at the time of this writing, director Mario Van Peebles is rigorously promoting his account of the Black Panther Movement, *Panther*. Yet, as Michele Wallace points out in "*Boyz N the Hood* and *Jungle Fever*," while many of these films are admirable for the ways in which they critically address black-on-black violence, black male homicide, and the statistics on black male incarceration, they simultaneously reinforce prevailing stereotypes of black women, especially black mothers. Arguing that *Boyz N the Hood* and *Jungle Fever* (and, by extension, other works by these now-influential black filmmakers) "demonize" black female sexuality (130) by securing all the female characters into predictable (and nearly invisible) roles, Wallace concludes that the message of the "New Jack black cinema" (Goldstein 294) is formulaic: "The boys who don't have fathers fail. The boys who do have fathers succeed" (125). In other words, the black mother and her role in the family is insignificant.

One is left wondering what black female filmmakers would contribute to the dialogue about contemporary African American life, but critics have long lamented their invisibility.[10] One notable exception is Julie Dash, whose 1991 film *Daughters of the Dust*, an historical account of an extended black family living on the Sea Islands off the South Carolina coast, thematically resembles much contemporary literature by black women. The words of the unborn child who narrates much of *Daughters of the Dust* apply both to

Dash and to the black women writers with whom she shares a kinship: "We are the children of those who chose to survive." Of her purpose Dash says, "I want to show black families, particularly black women, as we have never seen them before. I want to touch something inside of each black person that sees it, some part of them that's never been touched before" (Goldstein 295).

It is through their explorations of the subject of family that the writers of the neo-slave narratives contribute to popular culture. Like Dash, they want to "show black families," and to do so they have returned to the past to demonstrate that the black American family does have stable roots and that the black American family in slavery was no less a family.[11] As observers of contemporary culture decry the loss of traditional family values and proclaim the death of the American family,[12] particularly among minority cultures, writers such as Williams, Morrison, and Cooper are encouraging the contemporary black family by celebrating the heroic status of the enslaved mother, a model of inspiration for all black women today.

There is ample motivation for such an endeavor. In addition to providing a counterbalance to Haley's portrayal of American slavery as I have already illustrated, contemporary neo-slave narratives may also provide something of an antidote to the messages of controversial Nation of Islam leader Louis Farrakhan. Known for his advocacy of black solidarity, self-reliance, and independence and his anti-welfare, pro-rehabilitation viewpoints,[13] Farrakhan is perhaps most effective in tapping into the frustrated rage experienced by young inner-city black males looking for an outlet for their anger at white society. To his critics, however, Farrakhan is a mouthpiece for dangerously divisive racism, a man whose favorite scapegoat is the Jewish American, and a leader who misrepresents, even distorts, historical circumstances to suit his purpose. In one of his boldest declarations, he has alleged that contemporary African American society lacks family values because of the historical experience of slavery. This argument, correlating the demise of family values and the institution of slavery, is one such instance of historical distortion; his conclusions are demeaning to all African Americans, but particularly so to the large segment of black female heads-of-household.

Indeed, the statistics representing the economic and social condition of the black family in America, particularly beginning in the 1980s, are grim.[14] They are especially relevant to this project both because of black women's long-entrenched role as bearers of tradition and because so many black families are headed by women. Poverty among black women has grown at an alarming rate. According to research done by Patricia Hill Collins for *Black Feminist Thought: Knowledge, Consciousness, and the Politics of Empowerment*:

In 1985, 50% of Black families headed by women were below the official poverty line (U.S. Department of Commerce 1986). The situation is more extreme for young African American women. In 1986, 86% of families headed by Black women between the ages of 15 and 24 lived below the poverty line. (64)

Additionally, at this time black unemployment rates were double those of whites, one of every three blacks lived below the official poverty line, as compared to one of every ten whites, and median black family income represented 56 percent of median white family income (59). Inextricably linked to such economic oppression is social stratification, resulting in substandard housing, fewer educational opportunities, and the least desirable jobs, jobs that pay minimum wage and offer few benefits and little room for advancement. Thus trapped in a vicious cycle of poverty and oppression, individuals may respond in one of two ways—they may choose either to succumb or to resist.[15]

Resistance has long been the key to survival for marginalized peoples. In the African American community, this is best exemplified by the enslaved mother. There is every indication that these women loved and nurtured their children, even those conceived by force, no less than did free women. The very attempt to mother under the conditions of slavery, when the demand was merely to produce children to augment the master's labor force and when the awareness that those children could be sold at the master's whim was an everyday reality, was a heroic act. Enslaved women resisted in other ways as well—by learning to read and sometimes tutoring their children, by instilling in their children a sense of self-worth that served to contradict their enslaved condition, by trying to keep their families together, by serving as othermothers to slave children separated from their own mothers, by developing extended kin networks to provide and receive support, encouragement, and everyday assistance, and even sometimes by engaging in violence, as in the case of Margaret Garner.

Many of the strategies contemporary black women writers have discovered or imagined are applicable in today's society, particularly to lower-class single mothers. Today's black women can follow the lead of their enslaved foremothers and speak about their experiences in a racist and sexist society to their children, thus socializing them to the realities of life in America by providing an invaluable set of survival skills. Also, Patricia Hill Collins notes with interest the rise in community-based child care in neighborhoods plagued by gang violence, crack cocaine, birth defects, child abuse, and parental neglect. By assuming some share of responsibility for local children currently without stable home lives, othermothers both serve as role models for troubled mothers who may be willing to change their lives as a result of the examples before them and also ensure the survival of the community by taking care of its youngest members.

As bell hooks argues in *Talking Back: Thinking Feminist, Thinking Black*, "Oppressed people resist by identifying themselves as subjects, by defining their reality, shaping their new identity, naming their history, telling their story" (45). In other words, the act of self-empowerment is an act of resistance, and this is precisely how contemporary black women writers have expanded on the tradition their foremothers began. Whereas in Frances Harper's day the mere act of penning the story of Iola Leroy might be viewed as an act of resistance, today's authors are much more involved in active resistance, advocating the need for the black woman to allow her heritage to empower her. In doing so, she becomes an active agent in revising how society perceives her. It must be acknowledged that many of those most in need of the rich source of inspiration that can come from recognizing the heroic stature of the nineteenth-century enslaved mother will never have the opportunity to read works like *Dessa Rose* and *Beloved*; however, I am arguing that the effect of the neo-slave narrative as it is being shaped by contemporary black women writers is web-like, reaching beyond the reading public and joining with other positive depictions of black women to create a compelling sphere of influence. Black women have been struggling towards that revolution since the time of their enslavement; contemporary black women writers indicate that the time of revolution is now, and the source of revolution is the powerful past that is finally being claimed.

It is Zora Neale Hurston, through the voice of Nanny in *Their Eyes Were Watching God*, who has best articulated the black woman's place in history: "De nigger woman is de mule uh de world" (14). Labor market victimization of black women is as old as slavery, and contemporary black women writers, who may well view the economic and social conditions affecting many of their sisters of color as a twentieth-century form of slavery, keenly perceived the appropriateness of resurrecting the slave narrative genre; the double oppression of racism and sexism remains today. However, as Collins points out, "Fully human women are less easily exploited" (*Black Feminist Thought* 43). The neo-slave narrative as shaped by black women writers who pay particular attention to the enslaved woman's gender and her role in the family becomes, then, a powerful tool in assisting contemporary black women to resist marginalization. bell hooks argues that "While novels like *Dessa Rose* or *Beloved* evoke the passion of trauma during slavery as it carries over into black life when that institution is long gone, these works don't necessarily chart a healing journey that is immediately applicable to contemporary black life" (*Yearning* 226); nevertheless, they *do* provide alternatives to these negative images of black women presented to American society by the mass media and perpetuated by stereotypes. When black women look to the past as a source of pride, they are able to recover a sense of wholeness both in themselves and in their history.

Contemporary novelist and short story writer Barbara Neely identifies the significance of the neo-slave narrative when she says,

I've always said that probably our major difficulty in this country as black people is not what is happening to us externally, but what is and is not happening to us internally, beginning with a serious emotional exploration of slavery and what it has meant in reference to our perception of the world—the ways in which we raise our children, the way we manage our relationships, all of that. There is this huge and festering sore within all of us that we won't even get near, let alone feel. And then comes *Beloved.* (Carroll *Red Clay* 182–83)

What Neely articulates is a sense of survivor guilt that twentieth-century blacks, particularly those who are knowledgeable about their history, carry with them as a legacy of enslavement.[16] The neo-slave narrative writers are the first to make a conscious effort to break the silence of the past, to speak about the atrocities of slavery and to try to understand. Possibly even, in the true spirit of black women's creativity, they are trying to find something beautiful in it. As early as 1972 Alice Walker recognized the potential of the subject matter that black women writers are only now beginning to explore:

[T]here is not simply a new world to be gained, there is an old world that must be reclaimed. . . . [I]t is a great time to be a woman. A wonderful time to be a black woman, for the world, I have found, is not simply rich because from day to day our lives are touched with new possibilities, but because the past is studded with sisters who, in their time, shone like gold. They give us hope, they have proved the splendor of our past, which should free us to lay claim to the fullness of the future. (*In Search* 36–37)

The women writing neo-slave narratives are indeed concerned both with the past and with the future; their special talent rests in their ability to use the past and the treasures they have uncovered there to evoke the promise of the future.

To conclude, I would like to borrow a metaphor from Gloria Naylor, a metaphor she uses to describe herself but one that applies to all contemporary African American women writers, and particularly to those who are writing neo-slave narratives. Naylor says, "There is a rock . . . a certain kind of quartz that when you break it open there are all kinds of colors in it . . . it is a rock that is formed by fire, and when you break it open there are all these different edges and colors. And they are all strong" (*Red Clay* 165). Sherley Anne Williams, Toni Morrison, J. California Cooper, Gayl Jones, Octavia Butler—these writers have broken open the rock that is America's slave past and their own; they have discovered the strength of their color and the strength of their womanhood. These women *are* the rock—women of resistance who create women of resistance, both on the pages of their fiction and in the lives that their fiction touches. These women are shaping America's future, just as their maternal ancestors shaped America's past.

NOTES

Portions of this chapter originally appeared in *Womanist* 2:2 (Fall 1998; reprinted courtesy of *Womanist*, University of Georgia.

1. Christian does devote a section of her book, *Black Women Novelists: The Development of a Tradition, 1892–1976* (Westport, CT: Greenwood Press, 1980), to a discussion of Margaret Walker and the significance of *Jubilee*. See especially pages 71–73.

2. Bernard Bell, in his overview of *The Color Purple* in *The Afro-American Novel and Its Tradition* (Amherst: University of Massachusetts Press, 1987), is highly critical of Walker's treatment of Africa, arguing that she "conjure[s] up neither the texture, the tone, nor the truth of the traditional lives of African peoples" (266). However, for my purposes it is enough simply that Walker makes an attempt at incorporating into her work the importance of Africa and its ways into Celie's evolving consciousness.

3. Perhaps the best support for this point comes from Alice Walker who, in her essay "In Search of Our Mothers' Gardens," in *In Search of Our Mothers' Gardens* (New York: Harcourt Brace Jovanovich, 1984), sets the precedent for reclaiming the worth of everyday women— the mothers, grandmothers, and great-grandmothers of contemporary African-American women—as artists and valued sources of inspiration.

4. Not all black women writers acknowledge kinship in such a community; however, for an excellent example of the many ways black women writers speak about their importance to each other, see Rebecca Carroll's anthology *I Know What the Red Clay Looks Like: The Voice and Vision of Black Women Writers* (New York: Crown Trade Paperbacks, 1994), which includes interviews with numerous contemporary black women writers.

5. Both *Newsweek* and *Time* magazines devoted cover stories to the *Roots* phenomenon in 1977. See "Why *Roots* Hit Home" by Lance Morrow (*Time* 109:7 [February 14, 1977]: 68–77) and "Everybody's Search for Roots" by David Gelman (*Newsweek* 9:1 [July 4, 1977]: 26–35) for further statistics and popular analyses.

6. See *The Black Family in Slavery and Freedom, 1750–1925* (New

York: Pantheon, 1976). Gutman, in this landmark study, was the first scholar to provide an indepth assessment of the value of the black family in slave times.

7. Julia T. Wood develops this point in *Gendered Lives: Communication, Gender, and Culture* (Belmont, CA: Wadsworth Publishing Company, 1994). See especially pages 51–52.

8. I am using the term here in the way that Paul Gilroy employs it, to mean "the reconstitution of individual consciousness rather than . . . the reconstruction of the black nation in exile or elsewhere" (305). See "It's a Family Affair," in *Black Popular Culture: A Project by Michele Wallace*, ed. Gina Dent (Seattle, WA: Bay Press, 1992, 303–16).

9. Rap music has been surrounded by controversy almost since its inception, particularly with regard to the overt sexism of many rappers' lyrics. Sherley Anne Williams is one writer who has questioned rap music's content. In "Two Words on Music: Black Community," in *Black Popular Culture: A Project by Michele Wallace*, ed. Gina Dent (Seattle, WA: Bay Press, 1992), she asks, "Why, given the way we are so ready to jump on Hollywood, the Man, the Media, and black women writers for negative and distorted portrayals of black people, have black academics, critics, and intellectuals been so willing to talk about the brilliant and innovative form of rap?" (167). In her conclusion, however, Williams takes pains to point out that she is not condemning all of rap music, but is merely probing the implications of some lyrics. For an encompassing analysis of rap music and its implications for American society, see Tricia Rose's book *Black Noise: Rap Music and Black Culture in Contemporary America* (Hanover, PA: Wesleyan University Press, 1994). Her chapter "Bad Sistas: Black Women Rappers and Sexual Politics in Rap Music" is particularly applicable to my discussion here.

10. See, for instance, John Williams' article "Re-Creating Their Media Image: Two Generations of Black Women Filmmakers," *Cineaste* 20:3 (Summer 1993): 38–42. Ultimately, Williams celebrates those African American women who have ventured into the male-dominated world of film production and direction.

11. Both Bernard Bell, in *The Afro-American Novel and Its Tradition* (Amherst: The University of Massachusetts Press, 1987), and Patricia Hill Collins, in *Black Feminist Thought: Knowledge, Consciousness, and the Politics of Empowerment* (New York: Routledge, 1991), argue that the black family in slavery retained some of the hallmarks of African family life, which enabled them to re-establish and reinterpret traditions with which they were already familiar. This is perhaps best demonstrated in what both Bell and Collins term "extended kin networks," groups of individuals not related through blood but who nevertheless enjoyed all the benefits of being in a family.

12. What comes to mind immediately, although it is not the only example, is then Vice President Dan Quayle's remarks following the airing of an episode of the television program *Murphy Brown*, in which the protagonist decides to conceive a child out of wedlock. Quayle, while lamenting the overall loss of family values, was particularly concerned that the decision to air such subject matter on television would contribute to a poverty of values among poor minorities. The Republican Party received much criticism for Quayle's remarks, particularly in light of their poor track record in the areas of civil rights and social spending. For discussions of the backlash following Quayle's statement on family values, see especially David Whitman's "The War Over 'Family Values' " (*U.S. News & World Report* 112:22 [June 8, 1992]: 35–37) and Michael Kinsley's "Happy Families" (*The New Republic* 206:24 [June 15, 1992]: 6).

13. Much of what Farrakhan advocates is attractive to blacks; a *Time* magazine/CNN poll conducted in February 1994 revealed that two-thirds of 504 African Americans surveyed viewed Farrakhan favorably; 62 percent deemed him good for the black community; 67 percent judged him an effective leader; and more than half agreed that he is a good role model for black youth. For a thorough interpretation of the data, see William A. Henry III, "Pride and Prejudice," *Time* (February 28, 1994): 21–27.

14. The Reagan 1980s, characterized by previously unrivalled conspicuous consumption among middle- and upper-class Americans and simultaneously increased hardship for lower-class Americans, are generally looked upon as a period of setback both in terms of race relations and social opportunities for minorities. For a thorough discussion of economic and social conditions in the 1980s, see Haynes Johnson, *Sleepwalking Through History: America in the Reagan Years* (New York: W. W. Norton, 1991).

15. In the face of such overwhelming hardship, many underclass blacks may, in fact, look upon contemporary American society as a reincarnation of slave society.

16. bell hooks, in *Yearning: Race, Gender, and Cultural Politics* (Boston: South End Press, 1990), likens the experience of slavery to a holocaust experience, "a tragedy of such ongoing magnitude that folk suffer, anguish it today" (216). Interestingly, both Stanley Crouch, in his extremely negative review of *Beloved* ("Aunt Medea," *The New Republic* 197:16 [October 19, 1987]: 38–43), and Stephanie Demetrakapoulous, in "Maternal Bonds as Devourers of Women's Individuation in Toni Morrison's *Beloved*" (*African American Review* 26:1 [Spring 1992]: 51–59), compare *Beloved* to holocaust literature. Demetrakapoulous says, "*Beloved* is, on an historical and sociological level, a Holocaust book, and like much Ho-

locaust literature, it marvels at the indifferent and enduring beauty of nature as a frame for the worst human atrocities" (54). Both mentions, however, are brief, and my research does not uncover much scholarship yoking Jewish survival literature and African American accounts of slavery.

References

Adams, Russell L. "An Analysis of the 'Roots' Phenomenon in the Context of American Racial Conservatism." *Presence Africaine: Revue Culturelle du Monde Noir* 116 (1980): 125–40.

Allen, Kimberly G. "Family." *Library Journal* (December 1990): 160.

Alter, Jonathan. "The Long Shadow of Slavery." *Newsweek* 130:23 (8 December 1997): 58–63.

Aristotle. *The Complete Works of Aristotle.* Ed. Jonathan Barnes. Princeton, NJ: Princeton University Press, 1984.

Avant, John Alfred. "*Corregidora* by Gayl Jones." *New Republic* (28 June 1975): 27–28.

Bambara, Toni Cade. *The Salt Eaters.* New York: Vintage Books, 1980.

Barksdale, Richard K. "Castration Symbolism in Recent Black American Fiction." *College Language Association Journal* 29:4 (June 1986): 400–413.

Belenky, Mary Field et al. *Women's Ways of Knowing: The Development of Self, Voice, and Mind.* New York: Basic Books, 1986.

Bell, Bernard W. *The Afro-American Novel and Its Tradition.* Amherst: University of Massachusetts Press, 1987.

Bell-Scott, Patricia. *Double Stitch: Black Women Write about Mothers & Daughters.* Boston: Beacon Press, 1991.

Bergson, Henri. *Comedy.* New York: Doubleday, 1956.

Blassingame, John W. *The Slave Community: Plantation Life in the Antebellum South.* New York: Oxford University Press, 1972.

Bly, Nellie. *Oprah! Up Close and Down Home*. New York: Kensington Publishing Corp., 1993.

Bradley, David. "On the Lam from Race and Gender." *New York Times Book Review* (3 August 1986): 7.

Braxton, Joanne M. "Ancestral Presence: The Outraged Mother Figure in Contemporary Afra-American Writing." In *Wild Women in the Whirlwind: Afra-American Culture and the Contemporary Literary Renaissance*, ed. Joanne M. Braxton and Andree Nicola McLaughlin. New Brunswick, NJ: Rutgers University Press, 1990, 299–315.

———. "Harriet Jacobs' *Incidents in the Life of a Slave Girl*: The Re-Definition of the Slave Narrative Genre." *Massachusetts Review* 27 (Summer 1986): 379–87.

Brooks, Gwendolyn. *Maud Martha*. New York: Harper, 1953.

Butler, Octavia. Interview. "Black Women and the Science Fiction Genre." By Frances Beal. *The Black Scholar* 17:2 (March/April 1986): 14–18.

———. *Kindred*. Boston: Beacon Press, 1979.

Carby, Hazel. *Reconstructing Womanhood: The Emergence of the Afro-American Woman Novelist*. New York: Oxford University Press, 1987.

Carroll, Rebecca. *I Know What the Red Clay Looks Like: The Voice and Vision of Black Women Writers*. New York: Crown Trade Paperbacks, 1994.

Chodorow, Nancy. *The Reproduction of Mothering: Psychoanalysis and the Sociology of Gender*. Los Angeles: University of California Press, 1978.

Christian, Barbara. *Black Women Novelists: The Development of a Tradition, 1892–1976*. Westport, CT: Greenwood Press, 1980.

———. " 'Somebody Forgot to Tell Somebody Something': African-American Women's Historical Novels." In *Wild Women in the Whirlwind: Afro-American Culture and the Contemporary Literary Renaissance*, ed. Joanne M. Braxton and Andree Nicola McLaughlin. New Brunswick, NJ: Rutgers University Press, 1990, 326–41.

———. "Trajectories of Self-Definition: Placing Contemporary Afro-American Women's Fiction." In *Conjuring: Black Women, Fiction, and the Literary Tradition*, ed. Marjorie Pryse and Hortense J. Spillers. Bloomington: Indiana University Press, 1985, 233–48.

Cixous, Hélène. "The Laugh of the Medusa." In *New French Feminisms: An Anthology*, ed. Elaine Marks and Isabelle de Courtivron. New York: Schocken Books, 1980, 245–64.

Collins, Patricia Hill. *Black Feminist Thought: Knowledge, Consciousness, and the Politics of Empowerment*. New York: Routledge, 1991.

———. "The Meaning of Motherhood in Black Culture and Black Mother/Daughter Relationships." *SAGE* 4:2 (1987): 3–10.

Cooke, Michael G. "Recent Novels: Women Bearing Violence." *Yale Review* 66 (August 1976): 146–55.

Cooper, J. California. *Family*. New York: Doubleday, 1991.

Crossley, Robert. Introduction. *Kindred*. By Octavia Butler. Boston: Beacon Press, 1979.

Crouch, Stanley. "Aunt Medea." *The New Republic* 197:16 (19 October 1987): 38–43.

Dash, Julie. *Daughters of the Dust*. Kino Video, 1991.

Davenport, Guy. "Once More, a Little Louder." *National Review* 18 (October 4, 1966): 1001–2.

Davies, Carol Boyce. "Mother Right/Write Revisited: *Beloved* and *Dessa Rose* and the Construction of Motherhood in Black Women's Fiction." In *Narrating Mothers: Theorizing Maternal Subjectivities*, ed. Brenda O. Daly and Maureen T. Reddy. Knoxville: University of Tennessee Press, 1991, 44–57.

Davis, Angela Y. "Reflections on the Black Woman's Role in the Community of Slaves." *The Black Scholar* 2 (1971): 3–15.

———. *Women, Race and Class*. New York: Vintage Books, 1983.

Davis, Charles T., and Henry Louis Gates, Jr., eds. *The Slave's Narrative*. New York: Oxford University Press, 1985.

Davis, Mary Kemp. "Everybody Knows Her Name: The Recovery of the Past in Sherley Anne Williams' *Dessa Rose*." *Callaloo* 12:3 (1989): 544–58.

Demetrakopoulos, Stephanie A. "Maternal Bonds as Devourers of Women's Individuation in Toni Morrison's *Beloved*." *African American Review* 26:1 (Spring 1992): 51–59.

Douglass, Frederick. *Life and Times of Frederick Douglass*. 1892. Ed. with an introduction by Rayford W. Long. New York: Collier Books, 1962.

———. *My Bondage and My Freedom*. 1855. Ed. with an introduction by William L. Andrews. Chicago: University of Illinois Press, 1987.

———. *Narrative of the Life of Frederick Douglass, An American Slave*. 1845. Ed. with an introduction by Houston A. Baker, Jr. New York: Penguin, 1982.

Elias-Button, Karen. "The Muse as Medusa." In *The Lost Tradition: Mothers and Daughters in Literature*, ed. Cathy Davidson and Esther Broner. New York: Frederick Ungar, 1980, 193–206.

Elkins, Stanley. *Slavery: A Problem in American Institutional and Intellectual Life*. Chicago: University of Chicago Press, 1959.

Evans, Mari. *Black Women Writers (1950–1980): A Critical Evaluation*. New York: Anchor Press/Doubleday, 1984.

"Family." *Publishers Weekly* (29 November 1990): 48.

Fields, Karen E. "To Embrace Dead Strangers: Toni Morrison's *Beloved*." In *Mother Puzzles: Daughters and Mothers in Contemporary American Literature*, ed. Mickey Pearlman. Westport, CT: Greenwood Press, 1989, 159–69.

Fogel, Robert William, and Stanley L. Engerman. *Time on the Cross: The Economics of American Negro Slavery*. Boston: Little, Brown, 1974.

Foster, Frances Smith. "Octavia Butler's Black Female Future Fiction." *Extrapolation* 23:1 (1982): 37–49.

———. *Witnessing Slavery: The Development of Ante-bellum Slave Narratives*. Westport, CT: Greenwood Press, 1979.

Fox-Genovese, Elizabeth. "My Statue, My Self: Autobiographical Writings of Afro-American Women." In *Reading Black, Reading Feminist*, ed. Henry Louis Gates, Jr. New York: Meridian, 1990, 176–203.

Friend, Beverly. "Time Travel as a Feminist Didactic in Works by Phyllis Eisenstein, Marlys Millhiser, and Octavia Butler." *Extrapolation* 23:1 (1982): 50–55.

Gaines, Ernest. *The Autobiography of Miss Jane Pittman*. New York: Dial Press, 1971.

Gelman, David. "Everybody's Search for Roots." *Newsweek* 90:1 (4 July 1977): 26–35.

Genovese, Eugene D. *Roll, Jordan, Roll: The World the Slaves Made*. New York: Pantheon, 1974.

Gerber, David A. "Haley's *Roots* and Our Own: An Inquiry into the Nature of a Popular Phenomenon." *Journal of Ethnic Studies* 5:3 (1977): 87–111.

Gillespie, Marcia. "The Seraglio, The Plantation—Intrigue and Survival." *Ms.* (September 1986): 20.

———. "Toni Morrison's *Beloved*: Out of Slavery's Inferno." *Ms.* (November 1987): 66–68.

Gilligan, Carol. *In a Different Voice: Psychological Theory and Women's Development*. Cambridge, MA: Harvard University Press, 1982.

Gilroy, Paul. "It's a Family Affair." *Black Popular Culture: A Project by Michele Wallace*, ed. Gina Dent. Seattle, WA: Bay Press, 1992.

Goldman, Anne. " 'I Made the Ink': (Literary) Production and Reproduction in *Dessa Rose* and *Beloved*." *Feminist Studies* 16 (1990): 313–30.

Goldstein, Laurence. "Film as Family History." *Michigan Quarterly Review* 32:2 (Spring 1993): 285–95.

Goodman, Charlotte. "From *Uncle Tom's Cabin* to Vyry's Kitchen: The Black Female Folk Tradition in Margaret Walker's *Jubilee.*" In *Tradition and the Talents of Women*, ed. Florence Howe. Chicago: University of Illinois Press, 1991, 328–37.

Govan, Sandra Y. "Connections, Links, and Extended Networks: Patterns in Octavia Butler's Science Fiction." *Black American Literature Forum* 18:2 (1984): 82–87.

———. "Homage to Tradition: Octavia Butler Renovates the Historical Novel." *Melus* 13: 1, 2 (1986): 79–96.

Gray, James L. "Culture, Gender, and the Slave Narrative." *Proteus: A Journal of Ideas* 7 (Spring 1990): 37–42.

Greene, Cheryl. "Sherley Anne Wiliams, About the Impact of Her New Novel, *Dessa Rose.*" *Essence* (December 1986): 34.

Gutman, Herbert. *The Black Family in Slavery and Freedom: 1750–1925.* New York: Pantheon, 1976.

Gwin, Minrose. "Green-eyed Monsters of the Slavocracy: Jealous Mistresses in Two Slave Narratives." In *Conjuring: Black Women, Fiction, and the Literary Tradition*, ed. Marjorie Pryse and Hortense J. Spillers. Bloomington: Indiana University Press, 1985, 39–52.

———. "*Jubilee*: The Black Woman's Celebration of Human Community." In *Conjuring: Black Women, Fiction, and the Literary Tradition*, ed. Marjorie Pryse and Hortense J. Spillers. Bloomington: Indiana University Press, 1985, 132–49.

Haley, Alex. *Roots.* New York: Dell, 1976.

Hall, Stuart. "What Is This 'Black' in Black Popular Culture?" *Social Justice* 20: 1–2 (Spring-Summer 1993): 104–14.

Harris, Janice. "Gayl Jones' *Corregidora.*" *Frontiers: A Journal of Women's Studies* 5:3 (1980): 1–5.

Harris, Trudier. *Fiction and Folklore: The Novels of Toni Morrison.* Knoxville: University of Tennessee Press, 1991, 151–83.

———. "Of Mother Love and Demons." *Callaloo* 11 (Spring 1988): 387–89.

———. "Toni Morrison: Solo Flight Through Literature into History." *World Literature Today* 68:1 (Winter 1994): 9–14.

Harrison, Elizabeth Jane. "Sherley Williams's Post-Pastoral Vision: *Dessa Rose.*" In *Female Pastoral: Women Writers Re-Visioning the American South*, ed. Elizabeth Jane Harrison. Knoxville: University of Tennessee Press, 1991, 117–31.

Hedin, Raymond. "The Structuring of Emotion in Black American Fiction." *Novel* (Fall 1982): 35–54.

Henderson, Mae Gwendolyn. "Speaking in Tongues: Dialogics, Dialectics, and the Black Woman Writer's Literary Tradition." In *Reading Black, Reading Feminist*, ed. Henry Louis Gates, Jr. New York: Meridian, 1990, 116–42.

———. "Toni Morrison's *Beloved*: Re-Membering the Body as Historical Text." In *Comparative American Identities: Race, Sex, and Nationality in the Modern Text*, ed. Hortense J. Spillers. New York: Routledge, 1991, 62–86.

———. "(W)riting *The Work* and Working the Rites." *Black American Literature Forum* 23:4 (Winter 1989): 631–60.

Henry, William A., III. "Pride and Prejudice." *Time* (28 February 1994): 21–27.

Hirsch, Marianne. "Maternal Narratives: 'Cruel Enough to Stop the Blood.'" In *Reading Black, Reading Feminist*, ed. Henry Louis Gates, Jr. New York: Meridian, 1990, 415–30.

Hoffman, Roy. "Everybody's Mother's Ghost." *New York Times Review of Books* (30 December 1990): 12.

Holloway, Karla C. *Moorings & Metaphors: Figures of Culture and Gender in Black Women's Literature*. New Brunswick, NJ: Rutgers University Press, 1992.

Holman, C. Hugh, and William Harmon. *A Handbook to Literature*, 6th edition. New York: MacMillan, 1992.

hooks, bell. *Ain't I a Woman?* Boston, MA: South End Press, 1981.

———. *Talking Back: Thinking Feminist, Thinking Black*. Boston, MA: South End Press, 1989.

———. *Yearning: Race, Gender, and Cultural Politics*. Boston, MA: South End Press, 1990.

Hughes, Langston. "The Negro Speaks of Rivers." In *Selected Poems*. New York: Random House, 1959.

Hurston, Zora Neale. *Their Eyes Were Watching God*. 1937. Ed. with an introduction by Mary Helen Washington. New York: Harper & Row, 1990.

Jackson, Blyden. "Margaret Walker." In *Lives of Mississippi Authors*, ed. James B. Lloyd. Jackson: University Press of Mississippi, 1981, 444–46.

Jacobs, Harriet A. *Incidents in the Life of a Slave Girl*. 1861. Ed. with an introduction by Jean Fagan Yellin. Cambridge: Harvard University Press, 1987.

Jefferson, Margo. "Making Generations." *Newsweek* 85 (19 May 1975): 84–85.

Johnson, Haynes. *Sleepwalking through History: America in the Reagan Years*. New York: W. W. Norton, 1991.

Johnson, Marilyn. "Oprah Between the Covers." *Life* (September 1997): 47–60.

Jones, Bessie W., and Audrey L. Vinson. *The World of Toni Morrison: Explorations in Literary Criticism.* Dubuque, IA: Kendall/Hunt, 1985, 127–51.

Jones, Gayl. *Corregidora.* Boston: Beacon Press, 1975.

Jones, Jacqueline. *Labor of Love, Labor of Sorrow: Black Women, Work and the Family, from Slavery to the Present.* New York: Vintage Books, 1985.

Jordan, June. "Gettin Down to Get Over." In *Things That I Do in the Dark.* New York: Random House, 1977.

Joseph, Gloria I. "Black Mothers and Daughters: Traditional and New Populations." *Sage* 1:2 (1984): 17–21.

Kenan, Randall. "An Interview with Octavia E. Butler." *Callaloo* 14:2 (1991): 495–504.

Kinsley, Michael. "Happy Families." *The New Republic* 206:24 (15 June 1992): 6.

Klotman, Phyllis Rauch. " 'Oh Freedom'—Women and History in Margaret Walker's *Jubilee.*" *Black American Literature Forum* 11 (1977): 139–45.

Kristeva, Julia. "Women's Time." In *Critical Theory since 1965*, ed. Hazard Adams and Leroy Searle. Tallahassee: Florida State University Press, 1986.

Larsen, Nella. *Quicksand.* 1928. Ed. with an introduction by Deborah J. McDowell. New Brunswick, NJ: Rutgers University Press, 1986.

Loewenberg, Bert James, and Ruth Bogin, eds. *Black Women in Nineteenth-Century American Life.* University Park: Pennsylvania State University Press, 1976.

Major, Clarence. "In the Name of Memory." *American Book Review* 9 (January 1988): 17.

Marshall, Paule. "The Making of a Writer: From the Poets in the Kitchen." In *Reena and Other Stories.* New York: The Feminist Press, 1983.

———. *Praisesong for the Widow.* New York: E. P. Dutton, 1983.

Mathieson, Barbara Offutt. "Memory and Mother Love in Morrison's *Beloved.*" *American Imago* 47:1 (Spring 1990): 1–21.

McDowell, Deborah. "Negotiating Between Tenses: Witnessing Slavery after Freedom—*Dessa Rose.*" In *Slavery and the Literary Imagination*, ed. Deborah McDowell and Arnold Rampersad. Baltimore: Johns Hopkins University Press, 1987, 144–63.

———. "In the First Place: Making Frederick Douglass and the Afro-American Narrative Tradition." In *Critical Essays on Frederick*

Douglass, ed. William L. Andrews. Boston: G. K. Hall & Co., 1991, 192–214.

McKinstry, Susan Jaret. "A Ghost of An/Other Chance: The Spinster-Mother in Toni Morrison's *Beloved.*" In *Old Maids to Radical Spinsters: Unmarried Women in the Twentieth-Century Novel,* ed. Laura Doan. Chicago: University of Illinois Press, 1991, 259–74.

McMillen, Sally. "Mothers' Sacred Duty: Breast-feeding Patterns among Middle- and Upper-Class Women in the Antebellum South." *Journal of Southern History* 3 (August 1985): 333–56.

Morrison, Toni. *Beloved.* New York: New American Library, 1987.

———. Interview with Charlie Rose. Public Television, Spring 1993.

———. "Rootedness: The Ancestor as Foundation." In *Black Women Writers (1950–1980): A Critical Evaluation,* ed. Mari Evans. Garden City, NY: Anchor Press/Doubleday, 1984, 339–45.

———. *Song of Solomon.* New York: Signet/New American Library, 1977.

———. *Sula.* New York: Plume, 1973.

———. "What the Black Woman Thinks about Women's Lib." *New York Times Magazine* (22 August 1971): 63.

Morrow, Lance. "Why *Roots* Hit Home." *Time* 109:7 (14 February 1977): 68–77.

Naylor, Gloria. *Mama Day.* New York: Vintage Contemporaries, 1988.

———. *The Women of Brewster Place.* New York: Penguin, 1982.

Olney, James. " 'I Was Born': Slave Narratives, Their Status as Autobiography and as Literature." In *The Slave's Narrative,* ed. Charles T. Davis and Henry Louis Gates, Jr. New York: Oxford University Press, 1985, 148–75.

Page, Philip. "Circularity in Toni Morrison's *Beloved.*" *African American Review* 26:1 (Spring 1992): 31–39.

Phillips, Ulrich B. *American Negro Slavery.* 1918. Rpt. with an introduction by Eugene Genovese. Baton Rouge: Louisiana State University Press, 1969.

Porter, Nancy. "Women's Interracial Friendships and Visions of Community in *Meridian, The Salt Eaters, Civil Wars,* and *Dessa Rose.*" In *Tradition and the Talents of Women,* ed. Florence Howe. Chicago: University of Illinois Press, 1991, 251–67.

Ransby, Barbara, and Tracye Matthews. "Black Popular Culture and the Transcendence of Patriarchal Illusions." *Race & Class* 35:1 (1993): 57–68.

Rich, Adrienne. *Of Woman Born: Motherhood as Experience and Institution.* New York: Norton, 1976.

Robinson, Sally. *Engendering the Subject: Gender and Self-Representation in Contemporary Women's Fiction*. Albany: State University of New York Press, 1991.

Rose, Tricia. *Black Noise: Rap Music and Black Culture in Contemporary America*. Hanover, PA: Wesleyan University Press, 1994.

Rothstein, Mervyn. "Morrison Discusses New Novel." *New York Times* (August 26, 1987): C17.

Rowell, Charles. "An Interview with Gayl Jones." *Callaloo* 5:3 (1982): 32–53.

Rushdy, Ashraf H. A. "Reading Mammy: The Subject of Relation in Sherley Anne Williams' *Dessa Rose*. *African American Review* 27:3 (1982): 365–89.

Salvaggio, Ruth. "Octavia Butler and the Black Science-Fiction Heroine." *Black American Literature Forum* 18:2 (1984): 82–87.

Sanders, Scott. "Woman as Nature in Science Fiction." In *Future Females: A Critical Anthology*, ed. Marlene S. Barr. Bowling Green, OH: Bowling Green State University Popular Press, 1981, 42–59.

Schultz, Elizabeth. "Out of the Woods and into the World: A Study of Interracial Friendships between Women in American Novels." In *Conjuring: Black Women, Fiction, and Literary Tradition*, ed. Marjorie Pryse and Hortense J. Spillers. Bloomington: Indiana University Press, 1985, 67–85.

Sekora, John, and Darwin T. Turner, eds. *The Art of Slave Narrative*. Illinois: Western Illinois University, 1982.

Shange, Ntozake. *for colored girls who have considered suicide/when the rainbow is enuf*. New York: MacMillan Publishing, 1977.

Shinn, Thelma J. "The Wise Witches: Black Women Mentors in the Fiction of Octavia E. Butler." In *Conjuring: Black Women, Fiction, and the Literary Tradition*, ed. Marjorie Pryse and Hortense J. Spillers. Bloomington: Indiana University Press, 1985, 203–15.

Sitter, Deborah Ayer. "The Making of a Man: Dialogic Meaning in *Beloved*." *African American Review* 26:1 (Spring 1992): 17–29.

Skerrett, Joseph T., Jr. "Recitation to the *Griot*: Storytelling and Learning in Toni Morrison's *Song of Solomon*." In *Conjuring: Black Women, Fiction, and the Literary Tradition*, ed. Marjorie Pryse and Hortense J. Spillers. Bloomington: Indiana University Press, 1985, 192–202.

Spelman, Elizabeth V. *Inessential Woman: Problems of Exclusion in Feminist Thought*. Boston: Beacon Press, 1988.

Spillers, Hortense J. "A Hateful Passion, A Lost Love." *Feminist Studies* 9 (Summer 1983): 293–323.

———. "Cross-Currents, Discontinuities: Black Women's Fiction." In *Conjuring: Black Women, Fiction, and the Literary Tradition*, ed.

Marjorie Pryse and Hortense J. Spillers. Bloomington: Indiana University Press, 1985, 249–61.

Starling, Marion Wilson. *The Slave Narrative: Its Place in American History*, 2nd edition. Washington, DC: Howard University Press, 1988.

Stepto, Robert B. *From Behind the Veil: A Study of Afro-American Narrative*. Urbana: University of Illinois Press, 1979.

Stetson, Erlene. "Studying Slavery: Some Literary and Pedagogical Considerations on the Black Female Slave." In *All the Women Are White, All the Blacks Are Men, But Some of Us Are Brave*," ed. Gloria T. Hull et al. New York: The Feminist Press, 1982, 61–84.

Travis, Molly Abel. "Speaking from the Silence of the Slave Narrative: *Beloved* and African-American Women's History." *Texas Review* 13 (Spring-Summer 1992): 69–81.

Truth, Sojourner. "Ain't I a Woman?" In *The Norton Anthology of Literature by Women*, ed. Sandra M. Gilbert and Susan Gubar. New York: W. W. Norton, 1985, 253.

Updike, Edith. "Romance Novels Now Come in All Colors." *The Raleigh News & Observer* (17 August 1994): 3E.

Updike, John. "Selda, Lilia, Ursa, Great Gram, and Other Ladies in Distress." *New Yorker* 51 (18 August 1975): 80–83.

Walker, Alice. *The Color Purple*. New York: Washington Square Press, 1982.

———. *In Search of Our Mothers' Gardens*. New York: Harcourt Brace Jovanovich, 1983, 33–41.

Walker, Margaret. "How I Wrote *Jubilee*." In *How I Wrote* Jubilee *and Other Essays on Life and Literature*, ed. Maryemma Graham. New York: The Feminist Press at City University of New York, 1990, 50–65.

———. *Jubilee*. New York: Bantam Books, 1966.

Wallace, Michele. "*Boyz N the Hood* and *Jungle Fever*." In *Black Popular Culture: A Project by Michele Wallace*, ed. Gina Dent. Seattle, WA: Bay Press, 1992, 123–31.

Ward, Jerry W., Jr. "Escape from Trublem: The Fiction of Gayl Jones." *Callaloo* 5:3 (1982): 95–104.

Washington, Mary Helen. *Invented Lives: Narratives of Black Women 1860–1960*. Garden City, NY: Doubleday & Co., 1987.

White, Deborah Gray. *Ar'n't I a Woman? Female Slaves in the Plantation South*. New York: W. W. Norton, 1985.

Whitman, David. "The War over 'Family Values.' " *U.S. News & World Report* 112:22 (8 June 1992): 35–37.

Williams, John. "Re-Creating Their Media Image: Two Generations of

Black Women Filmmakers." *Cineaste* 20:3 (Summer 1993): 38–42.

Williams, Kenny J. *They Also Spoke: An Essay on Negro Literature in America, 1787–1930.* Nashville, TN: Townsend Press, 1970, 80–114.

Williams, Sherley Anne. *Dessa Rose.* New York: Berkley Books. 1986.

———. "Meditations on History." In *Midnight Birds: Stories by Contemporary Black Women Writers,* ed. Mary Helen Washington. New York: Anchor Books, 1980, 195–248.

———. "Two Words on Music: Black Community." In *Black Popular Culture: A Project by Michele Wallace,* ed. Gina Dent. Seattle, WA: Bay Press, 1992, 164–72.

Willis, Susan. *Specifying: Black Women Writing the American Experience.* Madison: University of Wisconsin Press, 1987, 3–25, 159–68.

Wood, Julia T. *Gendered Lives: Communication, Gender, and Culture.* Belmont, CA: Wadsworth, 1994.

Wyatt, Jean. "Giving Body to the Word: The Maternal Symbolic in Toni Morrison's *Beloved.*" *PMLA* 108:3 (May 1993): 474–88.

Yellin, Jean Fagan. Introduction. *Incidents in the Life of a Slave Girl.* 1861 by Harriet Jacobs. Ed. Jean Fagan Yellin. Cambridge: Harvard University Press, 1987.

Zaki, Hoda M. "Utopia, Dystopia, and Ideology in the Science Fiction of Octavia Butler." *Science Fiction Studies* 17:2 (1990): 239–51.

Index